ROADIE

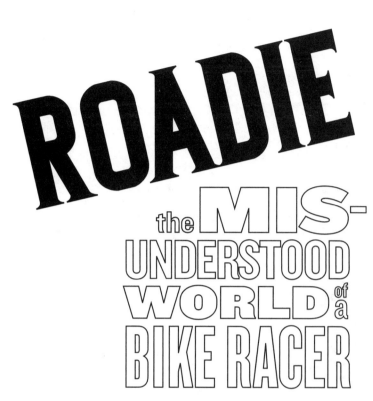

ROADIE

the MIS-UNDERSTOOD WORLD of a BIKE RACER

JAMIE SMITH

ILLUSTRATED BY JEF MALLETT

Boulder, Colorado

1830 North 55th Street
Boulder, Colorado 80301-2700 USA
303/440-0601 · Fax 303/444-6788 · E-mail velopress@insideinc.com

Distributed in the United States and Canada by Publishers Group West

Library of Congress Cataloging-in-Publication Data
Smith, Jamie O., 1960–
Roadie: the misunderstood world of a bike racer / Jamie Smith;
illustrated by Jef Mallett.
     p. cm.
   ISBN 978-1-934030-17-2 (pbk.)
   1. Bicycle racing. I. Title.
GV1049.S65 2008
796.6'2—dc22 2007044820

For information on purchasing VeloPress books, please call 800/234-8356
or visit www.velopress.com.

08 09 10/ 10 9 8 7 6 5 4 3 2

Cover design by Jason Farrell; cover illustrations by Jef Mallett
Book design by Samira Selod

This book is dedicated to the memory of my good friend, Suzanne Rustoni.

CON-TENTS

PREFACE

My infatuation with cycling, I now realize, goes much deeper than racing or even winning. The sport has substance. The legends, international flair, jargon, seasonal unions, and lasting friendships, the unseen strategies and the never-ending thrill of adventure. These are the Diamonds of my youth. —John Howard

That quote sums up the sport pretty well. I once used it when I tried to explain the sport of cycling to my parents. I was in college, and I had just spent $120 on a pair of new cycling shoes instead of spending it on food. They were pretty upset. They cared nothing about international flair or unseen strategies; they were concerned that I wouldn't make it through college due to either starving or spending too much time riding my bicycle. I was doing my best to defend my position, but the sport is vast, and my love of the sport is deep. I was struggling to find the words, so I quoted John Howard. Seriously, the quote says it all, but unless you already know the sport of cycling inside and out, you may not fully appreciate what it really means.

My college girlfriend didn't appreciate its meaning. After seeing her first bike race, she turned to me with eyes of stone and said, "To be honest with you, it looked like a bunch of guys riding around in circles for a couple of hours. I was bored out of my mind." I had taken her to see her first bike race hoping she would feel the same hook I felt, and while I adored her straightforward delivery, she made it clear to me that she hadn't had a good time. I sensed trouble. I realized that if I wanted to save the relationship, I needed to educate her on the finer points of the sport or allow the rift between us to grow.

Unfortunately, she was exactly right. At first glance, a bike race looks like a bunch of guys riding around in circles for a couple of hours. It's fast and it looks dangerous, but without some sort of commentary, she would have no understanding of what was going on, nor would she understand why everyone was so excited about it. At the end of the race, there was a short celebration. In her mind, they were celebrating the fact that they could finally stop riding around in circles.

Talking to a racer after the race probably wouldn't help her understand. Bike racers speak a lingo that sounds like a recording being played backward. The sport is full of jargon and nuance. It's also a bit quirky. To enjoy it as a spectator or a participant, a person must understand the many layers, and that means attending races, spending long periods of time around cyclists, and finding a patient teacher.

Or a book.

I spent eight years as a bike race announcer with Denver-based Event Services, a company that provided technical support (including announcers) to bike races throughout the United States. During those eight years, I was privileged to work with talented announcers, including Jeff Roake, Eddie Van Guyse, David Mayer-Oakes, Richard Fries, and Dan Mowdy. We all took our jobs very seriously because we were trying to explain a sport that is vast and intricate and subtle to people who had grown up with home runs, first downs, slam dunks, slap shots, corner kicks, and other simple sports concepts.

Roadies, in general, are such devoted fans of cycling that we want to share it with anyone who will listen and educate everyone we meet. We want to explain why we have ordered our lives around a sport that no one understands.

Eventually I decided to write a book explaining bike racing to the friends, co-workers, and families of cyclists. Too many Roadies have told me that they feel like outsiders in their regular lives, especially here in the United States, where professional cycling lacks the rock-star following it receives in Europe. This means the Roadie is missing out on great friendships, and friends are missing out on all the cool things that cycling offers.

As a bike racer, I had a very steep learning curve. There's a lot to learn. I also wanted to explain the hidden side of the sport to newcomers. The more they know about this sport and the sooner they know it, the more likely they are to get enjoyment out of it.

I have to warn you, though, that an explanation of bike racing does not proceed in a straight line from beginning to end. Consequently, my explanation may ramble and weave somewhat, but I hope you'll come away with a working knowledge of this amazing sport and your Roadie friend.

I have no intention of teaching anyone how to ride, how to fix a bike, how to eat, how to train for a bike race, or how to figure out gear ratios. There are plenty of books on the shelves that teach those things. I just want to teach people—spectators or first-time participants—the basics.

With few exceptions, everything I include in this book applies to men and women alike. I see male and female cyclists as brothers and sisters in a big extended family, and I don't exclude anyone from my explanations. For simplicity's sake, though, I've used masculine pronouns throughout. I worried about this until seven-time national champion Karen Bliss assured me that "bike racing is bike racing. We're all one big group of people."

The book is called *Roadie* because my goal is to make accessible this very cool sport called bike racing, specifically, *road* cycling. Forgive me if I don't write one paragraph about mountain biking. That's a different sport, and it falls upon mountain bikers to tell you about their thing. I don't know much about mountain biking, so I shouldn't be the one to write about it.

I know road cycling pretty well, and I think you'll like it too once you're familiar with it—either as a spectator or as a participant soon to be immersed in this world (if you aren't already).

ACKNOWLEDGMENTS

For someone who dreaded having to write a five-page paper in college, the idea of writing a book should have been more daunting than it was. Instead, it was quite easy, mainly because of the friends I have in and out of the sport of bike racing. You may or may not know who they are, but if you enjoy reading this book, then they are the people who deserve your thanks: Paul Alman, Jeff Noftz, Louise Kasl, Jeff Roake, Gypsy Patton, Beth Wren-Estes, Chuck Hodge, Sarah Stewart, George Bellairs, Bonnie, Paul, C.J., and Krystal Karas, John Sammut, Erica Blake, Richard Fries, Danielle Vacanti, Vicki Goldsmith, Leah Kucharek, Karen, Olivia, and Tim Joyce, Jason Dale, Jay Baumeister, Frankie Andreu, Lynay Smith, Margaret Casey, Joe Matthews, the Flying Rhino Cycling Club, members of bikeforums.net, and Roadies everywhere.

This writing project received crucial support from Renee Jardine. Were it not for her belief in this book, you would be staring at blank pages.

A special thanks to my family. If you find this book amusing, the Smith farm in Davisburg is where it started.

And to the 2002 Detroit Tigers with a record of 55-106 for providing me with a quiet place to sit and write: Section 326.

PART ONE
A TASTE OF THE GOOD LIFE

1. Riders Ready

THE FIRST LAYER

I can recall the exact moment I got hooked on the sport of bike racing. It was 1968, and I was eight years old. My cousin brought his ten-speed racing bike to my grand-mother's house one summer day. It was the most foreign thing I had ever seen, with its crazy handlebars, skinny tires, tiny seat, and angry-looking cogs. Everyone in my neighborhood rode Schwinn Sting-Ray bikes, so I stood awestruck in the driveway and looked at that bike like it was from Mars. And though the top of my head barely came up to the tip of the saddle, I knew right then and there that this thing "fit" me.

Most Roadies can recall the moment they first felt the hook of cycling. For many, it's a defining moment in their life.

Many come to bike racing after trying every other sport under the sun in search of one that fits their abilities and temperament. I excelled in Little League baseball and was destined for stardom until I stood at the plate at age eleven and watched the first curveball swoosh by me. I thought it was the most diabolical tactic ever imagined. (I later learned that a curveball is small potatoes compared to some of the tactics cyclists use.) I never got the hang of the game after that.

One of the coolest aspects of bike racing is that it has no limits. Unlike football or basketball, bike racing doesn't demand a certain physique for success. Baseball, tennis, and golf all require hand-eye coordination; cycling doesn't. Unlike running, cycling is easy on the joints. While swimming can take you to the other end of the pool and back, cycling can begin at the end of your driveway and take you to the other side of the country. Unlike soccer/baseball/football/basketball, bike racing has no bench to sit on. No coach is ever going to tell you that you're not good enough, big enough, or fast enough to compete. Your performance is a direct reflection on your dedication to the sport.

I'm not saying it's better than any other sport. Well, actually, that's exactly what I'm saying. Given the opportunity, I'd buy a network of radio stations and broadcast my message daily. The sport is expensive, dangerous, time-consuming, mentally draining, emotionally exhausting, and physically demanding, and it permeates every aspect of a Roadie's life (or lack thereof) off the bike. And it's awesome.

From an aesthetic standpoint, bike racing is a gorgeous sport—a blur of color, circles, triangles, and human forms pleasing to the eye. The ever-changing shape of the pack as it winds its way through a race is mesmerizing. From a historical standpoint, it's loaded with epic battles, heroic efforts, dynamic personalities, and plenty of pathos and human suffering. From a strategic standpoint, the tactics can be incredibly simple or mind-bogglingly complex. And from a lifestyle standpoint, it's a tough, demanding, grueling, scientific, technical, and oddly sexy sport full of sacrifice, dedication, and some really cool toys.

Though described by many as a "rolling chess game," a bike race is much more than that. I would describe it as a chess game, boxing match, and stampede disguised as a sport encompassed by a lifestyle surrounded by a community on a never-ending road trip to the brink of bankruptcy.

Compared with other sports, bike racing is an all-engrossing coil that simultaneously gives life and sucks it back out of its participants. And vice versa. One can dabble in tennis, golf, softball, basketball, and other sports. There is no dabbling in bike racing.

CLIMB ABOARD

Ask any Roadie to tell you the story of how he became involved in the sport of cycling, and you will hear one of several possible answers. Some Roadies have been racing their bikes since birth. Some stumbled on it accidentally. Some came to it as a means of recuperating from injuries in other sports. Some saw it on TV and wanted to give it a try.

For many, the seeds are planted early in life when they first learn to ride a two-wheeler. The exhilaration and sense of adventure and freedom can make quite an impression at a young age. It may take time for these Roadies to sift through all the other sports before coming back to bike racing, but those who truly have the cycling gene eventually come back to the sport.

My parents viewed my cycling obsession as a total waste of time and a distraction from my college classes. My friends thought I was just going through a silly phase. Later in life, my employer was afraid I'd get hurt and miss work. If someone expressed any interest at all, it was in wondering how soon I would give it up.

Every step I took farther into the sport was a step farther away from the mainstream. The gap between me and the mainstream grew by leaps and bounds.

SQUARE ONE

Let's start with some terminology. As an activity, it is called bicycling, but as a sport, it is called bike racing. We don't call ourselves bikers, so we never go biking. Instead, we go riding. It's a subtle distinction that Roadies tend to make. To us, a biker is someone who rides loud motorcycles and wears leather.

There is also a subtle difference between a cyclist and a bike racer. A cyclist is someone who rides seriously but does not necessarily race. Of course, a bike racer definitely races his bike, any chance he gets. Throughout this book, I use "rider," "racer," and "Roadie" interchangeably to mean bike racer.

The term "Roadie" is used to differentiate bike racers who compete exclusively on the road from those who compete exclusively on the velodrome (trackies) or on mountain bikes (mountain bikers). There are many riders who compete in all three disciplines, but there's no special name for them.

You're going to see the word "peloton" throughout this book. It refers to the largest group of riders in a bike race. We also have different words to use when referring to the largest group of racers in a particular race: pack, bunch, group, and field.

This will all make sense later in the book when I examine tactics. Obviously there are a zillion other words and phrases to learn, but for now, this is enough to get started.

AWARENESS

In recent years, most people have become aware of road cycling thanks to the Tour de France and the success of American cyclists such as Greg LeMond and Lance Armstrong in what has historically been considered to be a European sport. And though greater public exposure has raised its profile, the Tour remains a different beast altogether.

If you see a baseball game played anywhere in the world, it's still baseball; the rules are the same: Three strikes and you're out. Touch all four bases to score one run. Stand out in right field and stare off into space. It's all the same.

The same can be said for most other sports. The same rules apply no matter where the competition is held. But to watch the Tour de France and assume that bike racing is the same in America is incorrect. The principles are the same, but the types of races are different. We'll cover those differences later on.

A Roadie, on the other hand, is pretty much the same regardless of which type of race he's participating in, and it's easy to pick him out of a crowd.

SURE SIGNS OF A ROADIE

We all have hobbies. We all wear something on our sleeve that tells other people what we're into. Everyone in my office building knows that I'm the "bike racer guy." A guy down the hall displays a windlass on his desk, making him the "sailor guy." Everyone goes to him with boat-related questions. Another coworker has a full set of Star Wars figurines and bobble heads on his desk. I seldom see anyone talking to him.

I feel compelled to ask my coworkers questions about their craft/hobby/sport when I visit their cubicle, as they do when they visit mine. Usually, their activity involves a recent cruise, their home improvement project, or maybe a fascination with lighthouses. Conversely, the questions they ask me about cycling are pretty basic. Believe me, I've heard them all.

WHAT WILL OUR FRIENDS SAY?

What questions will they ask? Well, if they're going to ask anything, they'll start with . . .

> What's with the funky shorts?
> Why do you wear the funny shoes? Do you wear pads?
> What happens when you crash? Why do you shave your legs?
> How fast can you go? How many miles do you ride?
> How much did your bike cost? How much does your bike weigh?
> How can you ride on such skinny tires? Why do you have to ride
>   right in the road?
> Will you ever be in the Tour de France? How far do you ride?
> Have you ever raced in the MS150?
> Why do you do it?

These are all good questions, and knowing that all of my friends, coworkers, and relatives are still immersed in the mainstream sports, I appreciate their courage in asking them. Before I answer these common questions, I need to provide some perspective on the sport of bike racing.

ANSWERS 67 AND 68

I've participated in a lot of different sports in my life, but I can't think of any that require the high level of fitness cycling demands. It's one of the hardest sports you'll ever find. As I said earlier, you can't dabble in the sport of bike racing. Just being in "decent shape" won't be enough; success in this game requires tremendous fitness. To achieve and maintain a high degree of fitness, most racers must ride their bike no fewer than five days a week. Riding many miles is the surest way to do this. There are no shortcuts.

Oh sure, Roadies will use weight training, cardio training, and other forms of exercise to gain fitness, but the bulk of their training regimen involves sitting on the saddle and turning the pedals.

The fact that cyclists must spend so much time on the bike is probably the most misunderstood aspect of the Roadie's world and the cause for more hard feelings between a Roadie and his friends. It's not something we do because we want to; it's something we do because we have to in order to compete with the other Roadies out there who are taking steps to become stronger and faster.

- Many people take it personally, as if cyclists actually prefer to spend more time with the bike than with friends. They don't. (Okay, some do.)

- Many people assume that once the racing season has begun, there is less need to ride all those extra miles, as if the act of racing were enough to maintain the high fitness level. It would be nice if that were true, but it isn't.
- Many people think of cycling as a social outing similar to the golf course clubhouse, as if other cyclists were a Roadie's only friends. It is, but they aren't.

Racing and training go hand in hand; you can't do the first without the second. The counterpart to the amazing amount of time spent riding is the amount of time spent recovering from all that effort. You can imagine how you feel after riding a bike for five hours, so you can also imagine how much time you need to recuperate from the hard effort.

IT MAY SOUND ABSURD, BUT . . .

As a racing cyclist, I know that in order to stay competitive with the pack, I need to log fifteen to twenty hours of riding each week. That amounts to three to four hours per training ride in order to keep pace with what other Roadies are doing. Obviously, the mileage logged may vary.

I get home from work sometime after 5:00 p.m. and I immediately change into my cycling clothes, get on the bike, and go riding for three hours. I arrive home by 8:30 p.m. utterly drained. I do this four times every week from March to October. It has to be that way because each weekend, I'll be racing against ambitious guys who are serious about the game. I'll be racing against guys who don't even have jobs. These are guys who have nothing else to do all day but train and train and train some more. If I want to hang in with them at the speed that serves my ego's needs, then I have to train really hard. It doesn't leave much time for a normal life!

When a Roadie rides a lot and spends many hours on the bike, he needs to have the right stuff, the right clothes, shoes, bike, and so on. Now I am ready to answer the questions like Why the funny shorts? or Aren't those handlebars uncomfortable? and my favorite, Why the shaved legs?

WHAT'S WITH THE FUNNY SHORTS?

When I first started riding a bike beyond my neighborhood, I wore cutoff blue jeans. That was a big mistake. I get emotional just thinking about it. You see, blue jeans have a bead of cloth about the size of a marble located in the crotch area where four seams come together. Also found in that general location are body parts I want to protect. Nothing good can come from contact between those parties. After ten miles of those seams wriggling against my crotch, I felt as if . . . oh never mind. It was painful. Let's just leave it at that.

I wasn't ready for black Lycra, fearing the ridicule that would surely come with it, so I tried nylon running shorts. But after my first long ride wearing running shorts, I had severe chafing, and my bum hurt for several weeks afterward. There was nothing pleasant about that experience. Quite simply, comfort is the reason for those silly-looking shorts.

Some Roadies might mention the wind resistance factor; you don't want fabric whipping around like a flag. But the main thing is comfort. Comfort. Comfort. Comfort. A serious rider wants comfort at the three points of contact between him and the bike: feet, hands, and rump. Cycling shorts have a soft chamois pad in the butt. That's the main point of contact. Many casual bike riders fail to take care of that single contact point and therefore never get past the pain in the arse. As a result, they never fully enjoy riding, and their bike is then banished to a hook in the garage as if it's the bike's fault. When people see how tiny a racing saddle actually is, they immediately understand why Roadies put pads in their pants.

THE JERSEY SHORE

Add a colorful jersey to a colorful pair of shorts, and you have what Roadies call their "kit." The jersey attracts a lot of attention, so I'll give you some reasons for wearing one. It's made of a technologically advanced material that wicks away the sweat. It fits tightly to keep from flapping around in the wind. It has pockets in the back, so my stuff won't fall out. If the pockets were in the front, everything (cell phone, energy bars, tire pump, etc.) would dump out onto the ground as soon as I leaned forward to grab the handlebars. Also, these jerseys are usually colorful, which helps motorists see me. That's a significant point; being visible on the road is important when you're competing for a driver's attention amid the McDonald's, Blockbusters, and Starbucks of the world. The color of the jersey reflects my sponsor's personality, for I am a brightly colored rolling billboard emblazoned with the names of about ten different sponsors who have given me everything from the clothes on my back to the bike I'm riding.

I find it funny that other sports clothing can be worn in public. To me, softball uniforms look like pajamas, yet grown men have no qualms wearing them to Pizza Hut. I see kids wearing soccer uniforms everywhere. No one bats an eyelash. But try wearing a cycling kit to the supermarket, and you'll hear hearty laughter throughout the store. These clothes are not meant to be worn anywhere but on the bike.

LOOK, MA! NO FINGERS!

Many people are curious about the gloves we wear, and I guess it's probably because they appear to be a decent pair of gloves with the fingers cut off. They have padding on the palm for obvious reasons, but they have no fingers because you don't need them. The gloves offer a small amount of protection in a crash. They're such a small part of the whole picture that one paragraph is all they need.

"SHOE" ME THE MONEY

I love cycling shoes for the simple fact that they're designed for only one purpose: riding. They're expensive but worth every penny. They have a rigid sole that makes you walk like a duck, but their function isn't for walking; their function is for pedaling. The idea is to transfer all of your energy into the pedal stroke. Running shoes are so soft that your foot ends up absorbing a lot of the energy. This will also tire your feet and ankles in a hurry.

Another problem with running shoes is that there's nothing to prevent your foot from slipping off the pedal. Trust me, in the chaos that is a bike race, a rider wants to be connected to the bike. On the bottom of a cycling shoe, there's a cleat (similar to a ski binding) that locks your foot to the pedal so that you won't slip off and keeps your foot in the proper alignment to avoid injury. This connection is something the casual observer has a hard time understanding: Why would anyone want to be connected to the pedals? My short answer to that question is: Once you get used to it, you'll see the logic, and I promise you'll never go back!

When this shoe/pedal system fails, it is usually followed by immediate mayhem. Ask any Roadie to tell you about a time when he was in, near, behind, and/or witness to a crash that was due to faulty pedals. When you're sprinting at 35 mph, you don't want to lose contact with your bike. Pedals are designed to secure that connection, but if they aren't properly maintained, strange things will happen. We'll talk more about crashes later.

PROTECTIN' THE NOGGIN

Speaking of crashes, let's talk about helmets. In a crash, one of the first objects to hit the ground is the head, a place where we store all kinds of useful information, so it should be protected. The helmet's design has come a long way in the past fifteen years, but I still hear people making fun of it. I never understand this. Who really cares what it looks like? As long as it's somewhat aerodynamic, well ventilated, as lightweight as possible, reasonably comfortable, and ultimately protective, I wouldn't care if it looked like a Ford Pinto. Some of the early models did.

DO YOU REALLY SHAVE YOUR LEGS?

Once and for all, here's the skinny about shaved legs, a major source of ridicule for male Roadies. I'm not sure which of the following reasons is the most important, so I list them in random order. Feel free to pick the one you like best because they're all valid:

- *Post-ride massages.* Massage helps the flow of blood, which helps move lactic acid and other toxins out of the muscles, which in turn aids in the rider's recovery. When we massage our legs, we use massage oil and topical lotions that penetrate into the muscles to provide relief. It is much easier to massage a shaved leg than a hairy leg. Plus, if the oils are absorbed into the hair, they aren't reaching the muscles.
- *Road rash.* A common injury sustained in a crash is a huge abrasion on the leg. The wound will heal much faster if there's no hair to hold in dirt and debris.
- *Aerodynamics.* A rough surface area creates more drag than a smooth area the same size. How much this actually plays into a rider's speed is up for debate.
- *Rite of passage.* In any group of cyclists, a serious Roadie can instantly spot the not-so-serious Roadies. The telltale sign: hairy legs. A cyclist makes a strong statement about his dedication to the sport when he goes against the societal norm and shaves all the hair off his legs.
- *Cool tan lines.* Nothing screams dedication more than odd tan lines, and none are odder than those of a Roadie. These lines are well defined due to the amount of time Roadies spend riding in sunshine wearing their clothing in the same exact place on their body each time. These lines are more defined on shaved legs. By the way, any Roadie who claims he's never lain out in the sun wearing his cycling shorts for the sole purpose of intensifying the odd tan lines is probably lying.

Those are the most popular reasons a man might give for shaving his legs. I've been riding for twenty-five years, and I've had hair on my legs for only six months out of that twenty-five-year period. As you might expect, I've had to answer a lot of the same questions over and over again.

And that brings me to a question people ask me when they discover my shaved legs: How often do you shave them? The answer is, about once a week. Most

FEELS LIKE THE FIRST TIME

Ask any Roadie to tell the story of his first shaving experience. This is mine: I was home from college for a weekend and decided to have a go at it, so I bought a package of those cheap plastic disposable razors and locked myself in the bathroom. Two hours later, the bathtub looked as though an ape had been hit with a weed whacker.

It was late September, and my legs were freezing. When I got back to Northern Michigan University's campus, I felt naked. I thought everyone was staring, but nobody was. Then a girl in my physical geography class said she thought it was cool, and I instantly knew that I'd never go back.

Roadies shave up, not down. And we never, ever use our facial razor on our legs or vice versa. How far up the leg we shave varies from one Roadie to another, so I'll leave that to your imagination.

FINAL LAP

The piece of equipment that generates the most interest is the bike itself, and that gets its own chapter. No matter how complicated it may seem, always remember, it's just a bike.

2. The Bike

On graduating from college in 1986, I bought my first new car for a whopping $6,200. That same year, I bought a new bicycle that cost $1,200. (If I had been making progress in winning my parents over, I lost ground here.) In the summer of 2006, I bought a new bike. It cost $6,300.

Here's another little tidbit of information that causes some people to shake their heads in wonderment: The average Roadie owns eight bikes. Do the math. That's a lot of money tied up in bikes.

I must be average because I have eight fully functional bikes hanging in my garage. Some cyclists keep their bike collection in a spare bedroom. Some keep theirs on display in their living rooms. Because I'm trying to appear somewhat normal, I'll say that my eight bikes are in my garage.

In all honesty, I probably need only four. And yet I refuse to sell any of them. Each one has a different purpose, function, or story behind it. By definition, each bike is a road bike—not a mountain bike or a hybrid.

Take bicycle 1, for example. It's the newest, fastest, coolest bike I own. Bike 2 is very comfortable. Bike 3 is quick and responsive. Bike 4 is very light, and the geometry places me in the perfect position to climb hills. It's not the most nimble bike on flat land, but I have other bikes for that, so I only use this one in races that are hilly. Yes, bikes can be that specific. Bike 5 has knobby tires for use off road.

Technically it's a road bike, but I haven't ridden it on the road in years. Bikes 6 and 7 are old and heavy. Bike 6 is one I've had since 1989. I only ride it when it's raining because I don't want to get my newer bikes dirty. Most Roadies refer to this type of bike as their "rain bike." It's several years old, but we hold on to it for sentimental reasons and/or rainy days. Yes, I said sentimental reasons.

My rain bike is the bike that I rode up Alpe d'Huez (a mountain made legendary by the Tour de France). I bought it at 10:00 a.m. on June 3, 1989, at the Turin Bike Shop in Evanston, Illinois. I accurately recall every detail. As unbelievable as it may sound, in the cycling world, I am as normal as pumpkin pie.

Most Roadies have different types of bikes to suit the many different styles of riding. They choose which bike they ride based on the type of race or training ride they are going to tackle. Most Roadies believe that the ideal number of bikes to own is one more than they currently own. This isn't too strange, really. Steve Anderson, assistant principal trumpet with the Detroit Symphony Orchestra, owns nine horns of varying cost and characteristics. The more advanced your ability, the more varied your tastes become.

Whatever the style, it's important for a Roadie to have a bike that's better than he is. In other words, his equipment should not hold him back. That's easy enough to understand. An average guitarist will sound better on a better instrument. A chef will prepare better meals in a well-equipped kitchen. An artist will starve less with nicer brushes. The only realm where this doesn't hold true is golf. Better golf clubs won't make you a better golfer, no matter what the magazine article tells you.

CAN'T BUY ME LOVE

I'm going to catch a lot of grief from the cycling world for stating that, in general terms, the bicycle has not changed much in the past fifty years. Roadies throughout the United States will clutch their chests, fall to the floor, and gasp for air when they read that statement because it flies in the face of their reality, but for the purposes of this book—at least for now—it's true. Bikes have always been made of the lightest material available. The design puts a rider on the saddle who then pushes the pedals to move a chain to drive the gears to turn the wheels. No one has come up with a better means of propulsion yet. The wheels are still round. The handlebars are still bent like a ram's horns. The saddle is still painful until you get used to it. And red is still the most popular color for a bike. For the sake of this book, I'd rather you looked elsewhere for technical information on bike development. For now, a bike is a bike is a bike.

What *has* changed in recent years is that everything about bikes is lighter/stronger/stiffer than before, which makes them faster. Also, the brakes and shifters work a lot better than they used to.

What you need to know about the bike to better understand this sport is that a true racing bike is made up of several important parts. Each spring, when I purchase a new bike, I have two basic choices:

1. I can buy a complete bike that's ready to ride out the door, or
2. I can buy each piece separately and assemble it on my own in the privacy of my garage. (Actually, most Roadies perform this work in the kitchen with tools and parts strewn everywhere.) True Roadies prefer to assemble their bikes in this manner so that they can select just the right parts to fit their specific needs and desires.

Either way, the bicycle is going to be made up of different parts, and the best place to start an explanation of this process is with the frame.

When I tell you that I ride a Bianchi or a Colnago or a Trek, what I'm saying is that the frame is made by a company named Bianchi, Colnago, or Trek. The frame is simply the tubing that all the pieces and decals connect to. The frame builder may be located in a small shop in Italy with one or two workers who lovingly hand-craft individual works of art, or it may be a huge company in Taiwan with a legion of workers lovingly mass-producing hundreds of units per hour.

Not all frames are alike, of course, so a Roadie will spend a lot of time deciding which characteristics are most important. Steel, aluminum, carbon, and titanium are among the popular frame materials. Each one provides a different feel to the bike's ride and handling.

WE'VE ONLY JUST BEGUN

Now that we have the frame, we need to accessorize it. Get out your checkbook; this is where the dollars begin to add up. You're going to spend the rest of your life savings on devices such as brakes, handlebars, seat posts, pedals, gears, shifters, spokes, levers, and more. You've heard the phrase "additional parts sold separately"? Well, this is the best example of that axiom.

Some of this equipment—shifters, chainrings, brakes, and derailleurs—is bundled into a group. This is referred to by the Italian word "gruppo" (pronounced

GROUP-oh) and is produced by one of four major manufacturers: SRAM (American), Campagnolo (Italian), Shimano (Japanese), and Mavic (French). Roadies agonize over which gruppo to buy, just as they agonize over the purchase of the frame. I'll warn you now: This is a decision that may take months to finalize.

PARTS IS PARTS

Parts that aren't included in the gruppo must be purchased individually. The wheels, for instance, are sold separately. There are several companies that specialize in making wheels, just as there are companies that specialize in making the saddle, the handlebars, the stem, and so forth. We need to look at each of these pieces individually. A cyclist must wade through all the technical specifications to make sure each part is compatible with the other items.

The Big Three

The three specifications that a Roadie is most concerned with are weight, stiffness, and aerodynamics. Everything on the bike must be lightweight, since the lighter it is, the easier it will be to put it into motion. Stiffness is an important factor in the transfer of power from the rider to the bike, but it also dictates how comfortable the ride will be. Aerodynamics play a part, too. Anything that stirs up the wind will be shaved away, rounded off, and smoothed over. Those three specifications cause the price of the bike to go up.

I can't overlook the coolness factor. Some riders put a lot of importance on how cool the bike looks. But this adds nothing to its performance and only delays the purchase. If you'll be leaning your bike against the outside of a coffee shop, go ahead and give some attention to the coolness factor. It'll come in handy somewhere down the road.

By now you can see that acquiring the right bike is going to be a very complex process. In fact, it might be helpful for me to explain the bicycle in terms that anyone can relate to: the kitchen.

Several Ingredients, One Recipe

When you design your new kitchen, you can choose top-of-the-line stuff or you can be frugal and buy the low-cost stuff. You may start with Merillat cabinets or choose Mill's Pride cabinets, add a sink and faucet by Delta or Moen, install a countertop by Corian or Formica, flooring by Pergo or Armstrong, appliances by Whirlpool or Kenmore, dishes by Lenox, and silverware by IKEA. Before you know it, you have a

million components, including a Pampered Chef garlic press and a Williams-Sonoma dish rack. That's how it is with a bike. It's basically a frame with a million components added to it. For simplicity's sake, we call it by the name of the frame.

You already know the bike will cost about the same as a kitchen. I recently redesigned my kitchen, and I can't believe how much time I spent trying to decide between two different types of knobs for my cabinets. Well, hello! That's what cyclists go through every time they buy components for their bikes. It's expensive, and it's time-consuming. (Out of habits acquired from being a cyclist for so many years, I chose the lightest and most aerodynamic cabinet knobs I could find. I think they have some carbon fiber in them.) Fortunately, I have only one kitchen. Not eight.

Eye for Details

Some cyclists can name every part of their bike and give you the specifications. Take George for example, a friend of mine who is an engineer for a company that supplies automobile parts to Ford, GM, and Chrysler. George can tell you everything about his bike in exacting detail.

When Roadies such as George set out to purchase a bike part, they study the specifications, memorize the dimensions, and spend hours online getting cost comparisons until they find the cheapest one. When they take it out of the box for the first time, they measure it, weigh it, and run it through a battery of tests to verify that it's precisely what the manufacturer said it would be.

You might think I'm kidding. I'm not. Ask any Roadie. If he isn't like George, he probably knows somebody who is. On the other hand, some Roadies are a little less particular. To them, a bike is a bike.

Many cyclists can tell you a detailed story of their first bike, and how they progressed from a heavy, beaten-up piece of junk to a top-of-the-line, state-of-the-art beauty. George can tell you precisely what parts were on his first bike twenty years ago. A true Roadie keeps that first bike hanging in his garage.

WANNA TAKE IT FOR a SPIN?

People who aren't Roadies are always astounded when they take my racing bike for a test ride. It is very light and very nimble. I might also describe it as twitchy. They are shocked that it accelerates so quickly and effortlessly. Most ordinary people own a bike that weighs as much as their kitchen. Most people have a bike that has ten speeds but only one that works. On a racing bike, everything works.

A racing bike is like a racehorse that just wants to do one thing: go fast! So when a friend asks to take my bike for a spin, I usually spend ten minutes giving a warning before I let my friend ride away.

The seconds pass like minutes; the minutes pass like hours as I wait for my bike to return. The test ride may last only three minutes, but I imagine the horrible things that can happen to someone who is oblivious to the perils of speed.

But, minutes later, my friend returns safely with a red face and windblown hair in a state of breathless shock. Every single time. Without fail. And invariably, the first comment upon return is always this: "Gawd, those tires are skinny! How can you stand to ride on them?"

The tires aren't so noticeable when the bike is standing still. But halfway around the block and pushing a meager 17 mph, my friend looks down at the slender ribbons of rubber beneath him.

"Yeah, they're only 23 mm wide," I say casually. That's about as wide as your thumb. At 20 mph, the tire looks as wide as your pinky. At 40 mph, it looks like a strand of hair. After a while, you get used to it. And believe it or not, even though they're narrow, they grip better than a scared cat.

Most racing bikes weigh in the neighborhood of seventeen pounds. The reason you want it to be lightweight is obvious: to impress people at the coffee shop. Just kidding. The real reason is that a lightweight bike is easier to accelerate and keep in motion. Key point: Light equals quick; heavy equals slow. It's simple physics, a subject I never enjoyed in high school.

The next question I'm likely to hear is, How fast have you gone on it? I don't mean to brag, but my personal record is 72 mph riding down the side of a mountain. That's fast. But attaining that speed is easy if you keep control of your bike while relinquishing control of your nerves. It also helps to have a huge mountain.

On flat land, I once reached 61 mph while drafting behind a fully loaded semi. I once attained a speed of 43 mph in a sprint finish. Otherwise, I can hold 33 mph for about a mile by myself before I start to cry. In a pack of riders, as in a bike race, I can go 30 mph all day (as long as the day is only a few hours long). But let me remind you that I'm just an average Category II cyclist. The "big dogs" can go faster.

Next question: Will you ever be in the Tour de France? No. That race belongs to the "big dogs."

Next question: Have you ever crashed? Yes. But that's a different chapter.

BROKEN PARTS AND BROKEN HEARTS

Roadies handle bike repair issues in different ways. Some inspect their bikes after each use. Others wait until something breaks and then address it. Their bikes can make more noise than a peach pit in a garbage disposal before they'll reach for a wrench.

Bike maintenance is a complex topic discussed in numerous books, manuals, guides, screenplays, and doctoral theses. If you want to learn how to true a wheel, rebraze a dropout, or replace a freewheel, you will have no trouble finding instructions. All I can tell you here is that Roadies differ widely when it comes to performing their own bike maintenance. Basically, they go off in one of two divergent directions: fix or pay.

Some Roadies love, and I mean *truly love,* the process of assembling, disassembling, reassembling, tuning, tweaking, and repairing their bicycle. They enjoy the mathematical, linear, and finite structure involved in assembly and reassembly. The bike can go together only one way. There is no room for creativity.

A majority of Roadies thrive on this aspect of bike ownership. Achieving the Zen-like state of "master bike fixer" becoming "one with the bike" is what these Roadies strive for every time something goes wrong.

On the other side of town are Roadies who only ride the bike and leave the fixing to the professionals who work at the local bike shop. These Roadies can handle the ultra-simple tasks, but if special tools are required (and most bicycle maintenance does, indeed, require the purchase of at least one odd-shaped, single-function tool usually costing more than $30), they gladly pass on the opportunity.

These Roadies rely on the know-how of others because of something we call confidence. A Roadie who isn't confident with his own mechanical skills won't have the total confidence in the equipment needed when he's pushing the bike to the limit with every pedal stroke. It's very important to have that confidence! That's also why Roadies give so much thought to their bike parts.

Foggy Mountain Breakdowns

Not all repairs take place in the cozy confines of a workshop. Bikes break down when *they* want to break down, not when *you* want them to. Therefore, all Roadies need to take a page out of the Boy Scout manual and be prepared to handle the down-and-dirty repairs out on the road: flat tires, broken chain/spoke/cable, shifting problems.

To do this, every Roadie needs to carry a small saddlebag that attaches to the underside of the saddle. It should contain a spare inner tube, a device for pumping air into the tube (a small pump or a CO_2 air cartridge), tire irons (for prying the tire off the rim), a small ten-tools-in-one device that handles many tasks, and no less than $5. It's also good to have the know-how to fix small problems before going on a long ride. Out on the road with the sun setting or a storm approaching is not the best environment to learn a new skill.

The most useful tool will be the $5 bill that will buy cookies and Twinkies when you are faced with an episode of the Bonk. (See Chapter 5.)

Glue?

When I first got involved in bike racing, I refused to believe older Roadies who tried to convince me that I had to glue my tires to the rims of my bike. I was sure they were pulling my leg. The idea is ludicrous, isn't it? Come on! Using glue to affix your tire to the rim?

It's the absolute truth. To begin with, we're not talking about normal tires. A normal one, of course, consists of a rubber tire surrounding a rubber inner tube on three sides. The tube is tucked inside the tire, which is pried onto the rim using tire irons. When the tube is inflated, it is the air pressure that clinches the tire to the rim. For this reason, we call them "clinchers."

The glued tire (called a tubular or sew-up) consists of an inner tube that is fully wrapped in a casing made of either silk or cotton. The rubber tread is affixed to the outside of the casing. The casing is sewn shut (thus the name) and glued to the rim. I know it sounds weird, but trust me: This is not a trick. The only trick is the actual gluing of the tire onto the rim. This is, by far, the messiest task a Roadie must perform. Oddly, it is also one of the most ritualistic.

First of all, the glue will adhere to anything and everything. It is designed to hold a cloth tire casing to a metal rim rotating at high speeds under load. It's not going to let go. If it gets on clothing, it will never come off. Even the most seasoned Roadies end up with glue on their hands, shoes, clothes, and anything in the area. Several months later, they will find remnants of glue somewhere in their belongings. Despite the inconvenience, the handling and responsiveness that these tires provide are well worth the effort.

That Clinches It

In recent years, tire manufacturers have designed clincher tires that are lighter, more flexible, more durable, and much cheaper, which makes them more attractive to Roadies. Consequently, and sadly, fewer and fewer Roadies are going through the ritual of spreading glue throughout the house.

DID I USE ENOUGH?

There's nothing worse than descending a twisty mountain road at full speed and having the following thought pop into your head: "Did I put enough glue on my tires when I glued them to the rim? Did I let the glue dry long enough? Did most of the glue actually end up on my shoes and hands, not on the rim? What's the worst thing that can happen if I did it wrong?"

The worst thing that can happen is that the rims can be heated by the repeated use of brakes. Eventually the heat can melt the glue, and the tire can peel off the rim as the bike negotiates a sharp turn. Gosh, it's good to have complete confidence in your equipment.

FINAL LAP

Lance was correct when he came up with the title for his first book: It's not about the bike. The point of this chapter is that a bike is only as good as the rider who's riding it. That spells trouble for hundreds of exquisite bicycles. It also puts the onus on the bike's rider to supply the talent.

A Roadie can assemble the best bike ever created, wear the latest clothing, and have all the desire in the world, but only his first race can give him a taste of what racing is all about. And it has little to do with the bike, the clothing, or the desire.

3. The Lifestyle

In what pro sport do athletes show up for a game in a dirty, smelly uniform that's been sitting at the bottom of a suitcase for three days? Since this is a book about the sport of bike racing, I think you can guess where I'm going.

Bike racing is a sport that breaks some rules. To many, this renegade nature is part of the allure. The amateur ranks fall somewhere between refined and bohemian, lavish and spartan. And the pro ranks often suffer a similar fate. I've never heard a good explanation for this. People involved in the sport just seem to accept it. In this chapter I will try to explain how it is, not necessarily why. It's a good starting point to know that, as the John Howard quotation in the preface stated, this sport isn't entirely about racing the bicycle.

I am not making up any of this stuff, nor am I exaggerating anything to make it more interesting. I'll have to remind you of that fact periodically throughout this chapter.

DIRTY LAUNDRY

For lack of a decent place to begin, I'll start with riders who wear a dirty, smelly uniform to a race. Crisscrossing the country in a van throughout the summer with five other Roadies in pursuit of a dream will do that to an otherwise normal person. Traveling from race to race from May to August has an ill effect on a bike racer's appearance and hygiene. When a Roadie sets up camp at a race such as Wisconsin's Superweek, he usually has, at most, two or three uniforms in his possession. (A professional racer may have five or six jerseys provided by sponsors.)

By the fourth day of this event, Mr. Roadie will have soiled all of his jerseys and washed none. By soiled, I mean soaked in salty sweat and then dried into a crusty, smelly wad of high-tech fabric stained with the white marks left behind by evaporated sweat. The safety pins that hold the number will have rusted, leaving behind an orange stain.

If this Roadie is staying in a hotel, chances are it won't offer laundry service because Roadies can't afford nice hotels, which means he'll have to find a coin-operated laundry, which requires babysitting his clothes while they tumble dry, which means he's "doing stuff" instead of resting and recovering, which means he's wearing himself out in advance of the next day's race. No Roadie wants to burn energy unnecessarily, so the trip to the coin-op will be replaced by a more homespun routine: rinsing the uniform in the bathroom sink in the hotel room, hanging it up near the air-conditioning unit, cranking up the fan as high as it will go, and hoping everything dries in time for the next race. It is not uncommon for a rider to forget about his laundry between races, especially if there is a lengthy drive to the next race. When this happens, he will be forced to wear his smelly, sweat-soaked jersey to the starting line. A rider who has no hotel room may wash his jersey in the sink at a freeway rest area and hold it out the sunroof to dry as he drives to the next race.

A hotel is a rare luxury for amateur racers. Most riders look for cheaper housing, usually because they have no money but also because many bike racers are known to be tightwads afraid to part with a few extra dollars. The obvious irony is that a

SUPER Weeks

Superweek is a monster event in Wisconsin that the locals lovingly refer to as the American Tour de France because it takes place at the same time as the real Tour de France and resembles the Tour in that it visits a new town each day. It also attracts many European riders who aren't invited to ride the Tour. It consists of nineteen different races in seventeen days. (Yeah, I know what you're thinking: Why do they call it Superweek when it lasts nearly three weeks? Because it started as a weeklong event in the mid-1960s. Everything about it grew except for the name.)

sport as expensive as cycling is no place for a tightwad. Perhaps it is the expense that creates the tightwads. Usually the first thing to go is creature comfort. So the Roadie finds out where a onetime college roommate or some distant relative lives. Anyone who may have a spare bed or thick carpeting is placed on the maybe-they'll-let-me-crash-on-their-floor list.

LONG-LOST RELATIVES ARE NEVER LOST

"Do we know anyone in Vail?" I had to ask my parents that question when I was planning a trip with George and a couple of other teammates to a bike race in Colorado. None of us had money for a hotel room. We knew we weren't likely to win much with our racing skills, but we really wanted to race in Colorado, so we tried everything to make the trip happen. It's similar to a carload of fraternity brothers trying to get to Daytona Beach for spring break.

As it turns out, we stayed with my dad's second cousin and his family, and we had a fantastic weekend. We didn't win a dime, but we were treated like rock stars. When we left, they urged us to come again the following year. Those words are music to the ears of a bike racer.

When bike racers do decide to spend their life savings on a hotel room, it will likely be the cheapest hotel in the worst part of town with bullet holes in the door and bars on the windows. With four cyclists sharing a room, two will get dibs on a bed, and the other two will sleep on the floor. If the event requires two nights of lodging, then the two who slept on the floor the first night will get to sleep on the beds the second night, and vice versa. When other racers learn that their friends have splurged on a hotel room, they will ask permission to crash on the floor. They will be asked to either help pay the bill or pay for meals.

The most people I have ever seen sharing one hotel room was twelve. We took the mattresses off the box springs and doubled our bed space. The trouble with this arrangement is that Roadies insist on bringing their bikes into the hotel room with them. For obvious reasons, they do not want to leave them attached to the bike rack on the car in the parking lot overnight. Thus, a crowded room is made more crowded by the presence of eight to ten bicycles. If you put three bikes in the shower, you can fit a total of nine bikes in the average hotel bathroom. (A reminder: I'm not making up any of this.)

LIVING IN A VAN DOWN BY THE RIVER

When a hotel doesn't fit in the budget, the car becomes home for a night. Sleeping in the car, despite how sad it sounds, is a popular option for cyclists who do not want to spend a dime. Younger riders who have no jobs are willing to put up with anything in order to race their bikes. To them, sleeping in a highway rest area inhaling the exhaust fumes from 150 trucks is a small price to pay. I've done it. George has done it. In fact, George tells a story about the time he slept in a rest area on his way home from a bike race in Texas. After many hours on the road, he was so tired that he had to pull over and catch a few winks. Oddly, the rest area was only five miles from his house. Still, he did the right thing. Better to sleep in a rest area than fall asleep at the wheel.

The older a Roadie gets, the less discomfort he is willing to endure while traveling. Then again, the older a rider gets, the more likely he is to hold a real job and have the money to afford such frivolities as a hotel room and pay-per-view movies. Younger riders willingly endure any hardship. They love the activity enough to live like vagabonds in order to pursue their own passion. Who needs pay-per-view? They'll watch DVD movies on their laptop.

OVERLOOKING THE DETAILS

Imagine spending three or four weeks fine-tuning your body in preparation for an important race. You eat the right foods, follow the correct training, plan your peak performance to fall on a given weekend, and have your mind set on a certain goal. But if you forget to book a room and find yourself sleeping in your car, you are guaranteed to get such a pain in your back that you won't be able to walk in the morning, let alone race.

Some bike race events provide host families for riders who travel long distances. By matching up bike racers with local families who warmly open their homes to strangers, the race promoter fosters a community feeling. Families learn about the sport from their guests, and the riders learn a thing or two about the local area from their hosts. Hotels don't offer this benefit. Nor can they offer the home-cooked meals, the comfortable beds, or the cat hair.

This arrangement guarantees an increase in spectators at the race because the host families have a vested interest in the racers. This also extends cycling's reach into the community.

NO TIME FOR POSTCARDS

Roadies travel to race their bikes. Their travels can take them to Gettysburg, Chicago, Nashville, or even Orlando. Although they may be surrounded by national treasures, landmarks, centers of tourism, and natural wonders, most Roadies will not do a lick of sightseeing. It's not that they're not interested. It's just that they won't cross the street to see a landmark or natural wonder. Knowing it's nearby is good enough. If it requires paying an entry fee or walking, then a bike racer will not go near it. Roadies have a popular mantra: Don't stand if you can sit. Don't sit if you can lie down. In other words, if there's a place to sit, a Roadie should never needlessly waste energy by standing or walking.

For example, the monuments in Washington, D.C., are free of charge, but they require a great amount of walking. Chicago's Shedd Aquarium involves slightly less walking, but it costs money to get in. Neither one will be visited by a Roadie during the racing season. Museums are on the banned list due to the entry fees and the walking and standing that are involved.

Seeing a movie is on the approved list of activities for road trips. Walking around in a shopping mall to kill time is banned. Golf is permitted with a motorized cart. Trips to the zoo are allowed during October and November. In fact, all of these activities are permitted during the off-season, except shopping trips (there are no bike shops in shopping malls).

Going out on the town barhopping is okay during the season as long as the walk from bar to bar is short and as long as there's a place to sit in each bar. If the bar is too smoky, forget it.

GIFTS FOR THE ROADIE

Now is a good time to discuss gift options, provided that your favorite Roadie actually deserves a gift. Appropriate gifts for a cyclist are easily found. But the first decision you face is, Do you really want to feed the cycling addiction? By giving a cycling-related gift, you're putting your implied stamp of approval on the activity.

(My mother pondered this notion at length before walking into a bike shop on December 24.)

The next decision you'll have to make is between practical and impractical. Let's examine the practical end of the gift-giving spectrum first. A cyclist always needs certain expendable items. One item that comes to mind is cycling shorts. This is almost too easy—you can never go wrong as long as you know the correct size and the preferred brand. It's practical and also somewhat personal. I'm sure this is no surprise, but be warned that cycling shorts can be expensive.

Other items on the gift list include tires, inner tubes, water bottles, gloves, eyewear, energy bars, sports drink mixes, and socks. Roadies go through these items speedily and always need more.

OH, YOU SHOULDN'T HAVE

Some Roadies like to be surrounded by cycling. They want everything in their home and office to follow the cycling motif. They have cycling shot glasses in the cupboard, cycling ornaments on the Christmas tree, cycling artwork on the walls, and cycling wind chimes on the back porch. Their office will have a Tour de France wall calendar, a Discovery Channel desk lamp, a T-Mobile Cycling Team mouse pad, and a framed poster of Paolo Bettini. They already have cycling crammed into every nook and cranny of their life, so finding a gift for them may be difficult.

If you give the gift of a pet, say, a yellow Lab, you can expect a Roadie to name the dog something like Lance Arfstrong or Barko Pantani.

Cycling Shorts WEAR OUT

If your Roadie's cycling shorts don't get ruined in a crash, they will eventually become threadbare—in a place the wearer can't see. The first place that wears away is at the "plumber's crack"! Seriously. Due to constant friction, the area on the backside just above the chamois pad will wear so thin that you can read the *Daily Mining Journal* through it. Most Roadies have no idea that their bum is visible and it's time to buy new shorts. They find out when other riders announce it to everyone. You can spare them this great embarrassment by periodically inspecting their shorts for them. Do it tactfully.

Other Roadies have no desire to surround themselves with cycling stuff. These people are easy to shop for. You can shop at normal stores and buy them normal things. I suggest kitchen appliances that help them maintain their strict diet. Again, gift giving depends on whether your Roadie is deserving of such attention. For example, if he missed your birthday each of the past three years because he was too busy training or racing, then you may reconsider the idea.

NOT LAZY, JUST MEASURED

Roadies are not lazy. Riding takes a lot out of the body both physically and mentally, and recovery is as important and time-consuming as the ride itself. It may sound like I'm making excuses for Roadies. They do lounge around more than most people, but I assure you that it is necessary. Roadies can usually be found sitting with their feet up. But don't be surprised if your Roadie returns home after a 100-mile training ride and hops on the bike for a twenty-five-mile ride as a means of recovering. This is normal, normal, normal.

AUTOMATIC FOR THE PEOPLE

Most Roadies prefer a car with an automatic transmission. The last thing a cyclist wants to do after riding his bike for five hours is pedal his car. Working the clutch, brake, and gas expends energy unnecessarily and is almost impossible after a hard race. You may think that sounds ridiculous, but it's true.

On the other hand, bike racers, on the whole, are better-than-average drivers. Their awareness of where they are in relationship to others is an important trait that becomes sharpened by years of riding in the peloton. They can judge the speed of moving objects more easily than many other drivers because they spend a lot of time in a pack of moving cyclists. Bike racers also understand traffic patterns and driver behaviors because they spend a lot of time on training rides in traffic that poses a direct threat to their well-being. Wrap a human being in 3,000 pounds of steel and air bags, and he will lose some of his instincts for self-preservation. A Roadie, in contrast, is aware of all those risks. There's no such thing as a fender bender on a bicycle.

Also, a cyclist behind the wheel of a car can easily find a shortcut through town based on the countless times he has tried to find the quickest route to a quiet road. After a grueling marathon ride, he always finds the shortest and flattest route home.

FINAL LAP

As we continue this journey through the misunderstood life of a bike racer, please keep in mind the lengths to which Roadies will go in order to be a part of this unique world. Bike racing asks a lot of its participants, and as this chapter has shown, Roadies willingly pay any price.

Before Roadies ever race, they must train. The training ride is a world of its own, and I'm about to take you there.

4. The Training Ride

A training ride is to a Roadie what studying is to a first-year student in law school. If law students aren't sleeping, eating, or working, then they're probably studying. And just like the dedicated student who buries himself under a stack of books in a quiet corner of the library while his friends are having a good time at a bar, the bike racer lives a monklike existence of sacrifice, self-discipline, and solitude, spending most of his time on training rides.

There are no rules governing the miles a Roadie needs to ride. Some riders can get by with 100 miles per week; some require 400 miles per week.

NOWHERE SPECIAL

Most noncyclists find it mind-boggling that anyone would choose to ride 400 miles in a week. For a noncyclist, 400 miles requires an airline ticket. For many non-cyclists, a five-mile bike ride is a major expedition that requires packing a lunch and making three rest stops. Without some reason to ride that distance—a cider mill or a petting zoo or an ice-cream shop or a lifesaving medical procedure—the ride is pointless. Yet the average Roadie rides 250 to 400 miles per week with no particular destination.

Training rides are not about the destination. They are about objectives and goals. They vary in length and objective. There are 100-mile marathon rides that build strength and endurance. There are medium-distance tempo rides that build speed. There are hilly rides that help strengthen climbing skills. There are short rides that help develop sprinting and recovery ability. There are easy-paced recovery rides that allow a rider to recharge mind and muscles. Every training ride helps move Roadies in the direction of their cycling goals. If a training ride doesn't have a purpose, then it's time for the cyclist to get a new hobby because he is obviously just looking for an excuse to get out of the house.

The need to spend an inordinate amount of time on the bike comes from the high level of fitness/strength/endurance required to compete in the racing. Other sports are not as exacting in this regard. If you're carrying a few extra pounds, there's still a place for you on the softball team. You can be in ghastly physical shape and still win the Sunday night bowling league. Heavy smokers can sign up for a golf league without reservation. In cycling, however, if you're not fit, you will get dropped.

Getting dropped means you're unable to maintain the pace set by others, and they leave you behind. It's like watching a busload of classmates leave on a field trip to a theme park while you stay home to babysit your kid brother. Earlier I mentioned that crashing is a Roadie's worst fear. Getting dropped is the second-worst fear. Being left behind means that no matter what you've done to prepare, it's not enough. That's a bitter pill to swallow.

As already mentioned, a rider gains cycling fitness/strength/endurance only by riding many miles. Taking an aerobics class will help develop the cardiovascular system but will not translate into much of anything on the bike. Similarly, spinning classes at the gym are a good workout, but they're no replacement for the real thing. Lifting weights will help a cyclist's strength, but there's more to bike racing than strength. There is no substitute for riding.

DEAR DIARY

Most riders have a set schedule for their training rides. Many riders keep a training journal to track their diet, the weather conditions, their state of being, their total miles, and how long they took to complete their regular route. The purpose of a journal is to help riders spot trends, predict peaks, plot their season, understand their body, and mark their progress. For example, after a week of fantastic riding, they can use the journal to determine what went right. They may wish to repeat the

GETTING DROPPED

Let me explain something about getting dropped. Most amateur runners readily accept the fact that many of them will cross the finish line long after the winner has showered and left for home. Here's an excerpt of a typical conversation after a 10K footrace:

Hector: Hey Clarence! How'd you do?
Clarence: Great! I did really well! I finished in 2,748th place overall and 356th in my age group! I had to walk the last kilometer, but I was determined to finish.
Hector: Good job! That's awesome!

First, notice that runners have funny names. Also, notice how happy Clarence is that he finished the race on the same day as the winner. And Hector is supportive, too. That's really sweet, but you won't see it in cycling. Roadies would prefer to hang themselves from a bike hook in their garage than to get dropped from the main group in a bike race. There is nothing more deflating and disappointing than watching the field ride away from you. Getting dropped is the pinnacle of ignominy. Bike racing is not about "doing your best" or "setting personal records." Bike racing is about competing against (or at least keeping up with) the best. A typical post-race conversation between two Roadies might sound like this:

Thor: Hey Zeus, how'd you do? (Knowing full well that Zeus was dropped.)
Zeus: I got dropped.
Thor: What a shame. I guess you'll probably be selling off your bikes and joining the convent then, right?

formula sometime in the future. It will help if they know what went into making it happen.

Some journals are elaborately designed books printed and published for the purpose of documenting every detail of a training ride, ranging from the barometric pressure and wind direction to the rider's daily caloric intake broken down by grams of protein/fat/carbohydrates. Some Roadies keep journals that are nothing more than a few cryptic notes scrawled on the calendar. The complexity of a rider's journal is not a direct reflection on his ability to race the bike. What goes into his journal is.

I don't want to spend too much time discussing training methods. Instead, I'll focus on the nuts and bolts of the training ride and urge you to ask any Roadie about his training methods. Be prepared to spend a good portion of your day listening to the answer.

RIBBONS OF PAVEMENT

The key to a decent training ride is riding on decent roads. In a perfect world, that would be a two-lane road, smoothly paved, hilly, curvy, and scenic, with a perpetual tailwind and no automobile traffic. Picture the Pacific Coast Highway with no cars. At the other end of the scale is Central Avenue in Albuquerque, New Mexico, a street that is six lanes wide, flat, busy at all hours of the day, and devoid of scenery except for an occasional glimpse of Sandia Peak. Another example of an unfriendly road is U.S. 2 in Michigan's Upper Peninsula. It's a scenic two-lane road that winds along Lake Michigan and usually has a tailwind from west to east, but with logging trucks, RVs, rough pavement, a high speed limit, and an occasional black bear, this road is a cyclist's nightmare. By car, it's a beautiful stretch of highway; by bike, it's a ribbon of fear.

Those are the two extremes. Safe, smooth, scenic, challenging, and lightly traveled on one hand and rough, congested, boring, flat, and full of potholes on the other. You might think a Roadie's first priority would be to find a road that is safe and doesn't have too much traffic. Well, as far as I can tell, safety is not a Roadie's main concern. Cyclists often forsake safety in favor of a challenging route for their training ride.

"Today is Wednesday. I need hill training today, so I must ride on Route 37." Forget the fact that Route 37 has more traffic than Times Square; if hill training is what he seeks and Route 37 has hills, then a Roadie will ride it.

There is a man who works in my office building. He drives a red car. He has more dents on his car than the loser of the demolition derby at the 4-H Fair. He always drives too fast. Whenever he stops, his brakes squeal like a pig. He never looks at the road. He's constantly checking his appearance in his rearview mirror. He steers the car with his knee while looking for a CD under his seat. He talks to who-knows-who about who-knows-what on his cell phone all the time.

Whenever I go for a bike ride, I try not to remember that there are a million drivers just like him. He thinks he is the sole owner of Route 37.

ROAD RAGE

Of equal danger is the driver who either runs the cyclist off the road or just scares him. Some motorists, in their self-important hurry to get to wherever they're going, feel they have a right to punish anything that impedes their movement. By forcing a cyclist off the road, they are teaching him a lesson by putting him in his place. They show disregard for the law as well as for human life.

Many drivers believe that cyclists don't belong on the road. However, most states allow bicycle traffic on the paved surface of the roadway as far to the right as is practicable. Unfortunately, some motorists do not accept this, so cyclists experience harassment from rude, uninformed drivers. (In the unlikely event that it ever comes up in conversation, the Michigan Vehicle Code section 257.657 states the following: "Every person riding a bicycle or moped upon a roadway shall be granted all of the rights and shall be subject to all of the duties applicable to the driver of a vehicle by this chapter.") We all have stories of close calls and interactions with rude drivers. Ask any Roadie and be prepared to hear scary tales of close calls, near misses, and wild chases. You may never let him go for another training ride again.

Every Roadie knows that the best way to deal with a confrontational motorist is to smile, wave, and get away as quickly as possible. There's no good outcome if you engage an angry motorist: You will never have the last laugh; you will never teach the driver a lesson. Let's move on to more details about the training ride.

Training rides aren't easily defined. They take many forms but fall into two basic types: solo and group. I'll also mention some factors that can affect either type of training ride.

GOING SOLO

Get on your bike and ride four to six hours without talking to anyone. Go fast. Go slow. Go uphill. Go downhill. Push yourself as hard as you can. It's just you and the white line at the edge of the road. Ride past the beach and see everyone having fun in the sun. Ride past the campground and smell pancakes on the griddle. Ride past the golf course and count the hackers.

Sound like a TV commercial for a running shoe? Actually, it's an accurate portrayal of a Roadie's solo training ride. It isn't always therapy for emotional ills, nor is it a freedom romp through the countryside. It's simultaneously a blast and a necessary evil that Roadies must endure in order to reach the level of fitness required to compete at a high level. They will gauge their improvement by timing themselves over a route they've ridden a million times. They will keep one eye on the road, one eye on the cyclocomputer attached to their handlebars, and another eye on the heart rate monitor attached to their wrist. A faster time means they're doing well. A slower time means they'll go home and stew about it for a few hours.

The fact that the ride takes place in solitude is something a rider gets used to, just like the law student who sits in the library on a Friday night. We're sure that everyone else is living a rich, full, exciting life while we're out on a remote country road riding many miles alone. But we must get something out of it; otherwise we wouldn't do it. There are times when it can be a Zen-like experience. There are moments of exhilaration. It's not all pain and suffering.

ROLLERS

Speaking of pain and suffering . . . another type of solo training ride takes place in the basement during the dark days of winter when the roads are impassable and the weather deplorable. This ride takes place on the indoor trainer. Ordinary people call it a stationary bicycle. Many Roadies call it torture.

There are two basic designs: rollers and wind trainers. Neither one is fun to ride. A roller system is like a treadmill for bikes. It consists of three cylindrical drums (each about the size of a rolling pin) attached to a metal frame. The bike is placed on the drums. The drums turn when the bike's wheels turn. It's a simple device, and

it closely replicates the motion of bike riding. Riding on rollers requires a certain degree of balance and concentration. It's easy to drift too far to the left or right and suddenly find yourself hurtling across your basement. Proper concentration is a must.

Wind trainers are more stationary. The rear end of the bike is affixed to a metal bracket and held in a rigid upright position. The bike's rear tire makes contact with a single small cylinder attached to a turbo fan. As the cylinder turns faster, a great load is created by the device, increasing the resistance for the rider. There is very little about this system that feels natural.

Roadies generally have a love-hate relationship with indoor training systems. I don't know of any riders who like them, yet I don't know of any who don't own one. Few riders can last more than thirty minutes on such a system without going mad. But since their winter fitness depends on their dedication to riding on this device, they push themselves to ride as much as possible.

The trouble with trainers is that they are mind-numbingly boring. Despite the technological advancements that allow the device to interface with a computer, thus adding virtual reality to the training session, trainers remain a necessary evil. They provide the mechanics and motion of cycling without the pleasurable aspects.

GROUP RIDES

If I can ride 100 miles on a solo ride, I can easily ride 150 miles with a large group while expending the same amount of energy. Synergy enables a group of riders to ride farther or faster than any of them would individually. If I'm able to draft other riders, I will expend my energy at a slower rate.

There's also a social element to group rides that makes them infinitely more interesting than a solo ride. Over the course of a ninety-mile ride, a Roadie will have plenty of opportunities to shoot the breeze with other riders. Few Roadies will tell you that this is one of the best parts of cycling, but it is. It is one of those brother-hood/sisterhood moments of the sport.

On a group training ride a Roadie will develop and refine his bike-handling skills. A lone rider poses a physical threat to no one. Riding in a group creates a set of un-spoken rules, techniques, and etiquette.

Anatomy of a Group Training Ride

Group rides start in a parking lot. Much as they do on a race day, riders will gather before the ride, get their stuff ready, and spend time socializing. Socializing is usu-ally rooted in discussions of bike equipment. A lot of attention is directed to the

ROOKIE MISTAKES

Here are the mistakes rookies sometimes make during group rides, affecting those around them:

- *Overlapping the wheel in front of them.* By this, I mean that any portion of their front wheel comes alongside the rear wheel of the rider in front of them. This is a bad practice. If the lead rider moves the wrong way, we're going to be picking people up off the pavement.
- *Coasting downhill in the front position.* This may sound harmless, but it's dangerous. If those behind you are drafting, then they'll be coasting faster than you. Rather than force forty other riders to hit the brakes, you must push the pedals at all times.
- *Changing speeds.* Unaccustomed to riding at a steady pace, they disrupt the rhythm of a paceline and drive everyone else crazy. Inconsistent speeds also create a threat of collision.
- *Ignoring traffic laws.* They can usually get away with this while riding solo because their actions affect no one else. In a group, however, everyone must adhere to the laws of the land—or at least the laws of the group.
- *Failing to ride a straight line.* This may sound trivial, but it's one of the main causes for tension among a group of riders. If there is a "squirrelly" rider in an experienced pack, Roadies tend to be vocal about it.

rider with the newest stuff, who will be a popular guy, at least for that day. Most likely, someone else will have newer stuff tomorrow.

The group may consist solely of members from one club. It may consist of one main club and several interlopers, or it may include members from many different clubs. There is no hard-and-fast rule. Generally, though, if you aren't invited to join another club's ride by either direct or open invitation, it's considered bad form to show up.

If the ride is scheduled to start at 10:00 a.m. on Sunday, some riders will arrive at 9:00 a.m., and others will arrive at 10:01 a.m. The ride begins slowly. There's no rush. There's no fight for positioning. Everyone just rolls away in the shape of a large blob. Everyone wants to take advantage of drafting, so the blob quickly morphs into a definable shape as riders pair up into two-abreast pacelines. The pace is easy for the first few miles as the socializing that began in the parking lot continues. Riders talk about everything under the sun. Some riders talk too much, and some hardly talk at all. Neither is fun to ride next to. At a certain point in the ride, on a whim, some of the stronger riders drive the pace higher, forcing everyone else to follow suit. That escalation puts an abrupt end to the idle chitchat.

Fear and Loathing

Among riders, there is an odd fear of this change in tempo. Though fully aware that it's coming, riders sometimes dread the moment when "the hammer is dropped," for it means pain will be the rule for the next few hours. They might feel the first pang of fear when they drive into the parking lot. They may be unable to enjoy the easy pace for fear of what's to follow. It's not a fear of the unknown; it's a fear of the known: This-ride-is-going-to-hurt. They ride and train by choice, yet they still have a certain reluctance to follow through with their commitment because they know how physically demanding it is. But they always do.

City Limits

Typically there will be landmarks along the ride route that signal changes in the pace. On popular rides, every rider comes to understand where these landmarks are and what they mean. I don't know where the city-limit-sign tradition started, but it is accepted throughout the country. The locations of these signs are never disclosed to the new guy. Let him figure it out on his own.

Getting Shelled

Where races are held according to a rider's category as assigned by the federation, group training rides are open to all categories, so there is often a large disparity in the abilities of the riders. Within a club, this is one of the most important processes for establishing hierarchy. Those who drive the speed of the ride and finish with the leaders hold sway over those who get dropped or, as we say, shelled. (I'm not sure whether the word "shelled" refers to the effects of a mortar shell, as in blown away, or to what happens to a peanut shell, as in peeled away and discarded. Either way, it happens pretty fast.) In the end, every rider moves toward becoming stronger/faster/smarter.

THE ROAD to HADLEY

Baldwin Road is a nondescript country road near my house. We've ridden on it for what seems like a million years. It's lined with old farms and new residential subdivisions, and it leads to a high school and not much else. When our Tuesday-evening group ride turns onto Baldwin Road, things light up like a Roman candle. Without saying a word, riders start attacking left and right. The pace immediately skyrockets to 100 percent. Those who can't keep up get dropped. This crazy pace continues for five miles until we come within sight of Goodrich High School ("Home of the Rockets") and the school crossing sign next to the road—one of those yellow signs in the shape of a house with the silhouette of students walking to school. That sign is our finish line, and the sprint is as fast as any I've ever seen in a real race.

Whoever wins the sprint wins absolutely nothing.

After the sprint to the school, we mill about in the parking lot, drink water, and wait until all the slower riders catch up. Then we regroup and continue toward the town of Hadley. At the edge of town is the Hadley city limits sign. It is a small green sign that most people don't even notice, but every Roadie knows where it is. Every Tuesday evening, it is the scene of one of the most hotly contested sprints in all of cycling. That's how we think of it, anyway.

Just past the town of Hadley stands a giant hill that we lovingly call "Hadley Hill." There always has been and always will be a fast surge up and over the hill. If you are unable to stay with the leaders over the top, that's too bad. You'll be left behind, and we'll wait for you in the next town.

The ride continues this way for three or four hours with several more intermediate sprints and/or hill climbs before returning to the starting point. After getting dropped repeatedly, some of the weaker riders may split off to form their own group. The primary goal, though, is to avoid getting dropped and to be able to finish the ride with the leaders.

All Roadies have a similar Tuesday-night ride no matter where they live in the United States. In most cases, they are contested with the same fervor as the world championships. As such, these rides are usually referred to as the Tuesday Night Worlds. Remember, though, no prize money is awarded on Tuesday nights, nor are the roads closed to motor-vehicle traffic.

Throughout the ride, the slower/weaker riders live in fear of getting dropped. If they get dropped, they will have to ride the remaining distance alone without the benefit of the draft. They will also drop a few notches in the hierarchy. To avoid this, they wisely sit on the back of the group. They conserve their energy because they know they'll need every bit of it in order to complete the ride. As they sit in the back of the pack, they run mathematical problems through their mind: "We're fourteen miles from home, and we have four more hills plus two more sprints, at an average speed of 26 mph. I think I can make it. It depends on whether or not we stop for water in Shelbyville and if there's a tailwind on Airport Road. If we have a headwind on Airport Road, I'm toast."

A Few More Notes about Group Rides

If someone suffers a flat tire, an interesting thing often happens. If the victim is a weaker rider who has no chance of catching up, the group will likely stop and wait for him. If, however, the victim is one of the stronger riders, the group will probably continue without him and force him to catch up on his own.

If a rider has more than one flat tire during a ride, every other rider will feel compelled to criticize the victim's choice of tires/tubes.

If one rider in the group has to pee, the rest of the group will give him a ton of grief about it. They will whine about the disruption. They will make fun of the size of the rider's bladder. Still, when they stop somewhere along the road, every single rider in the group will pee. (Sometimes riders will pee while they're coasting down a hill. You heard me. They will not stop riding. They will simply stop pedaling, drop their shorts, aim for the pavement, and let it flow. And yes, this is also done during races. Ask any Roadie to tell you more.)

Roadies don't usually have bad rides. Of course, a ride may suffer from mechanical problems or rude drivers. If these elements aren't present, then chances are good that the ride will be a fabulous success.

Roadies will ride twenty miles just to get to the starting point of the group ride. After the ride, they will ride twenty miles to return home. As incredible as that may sound, it's quite common and proves that riders need miles to get in shape and to maintain their fitness.

A training ride is not a race. Oh, sure, it takes on every appearance of being a race in that there are attacks, breakaways, chases, sprints, and fluctuations in speed. The one element of racing that's missing is blocking. Since there's nothing at stake, you're free to chase breakaways until your legs fall off. Nobody's going to stand in your way.

WIND

There is simply nothing like a tailwind to make you feel like you're Superman. A good tailwind acts as a turbocharger. Suddenly Roadies are faster with the same amount of output. If speed is what attracts many Roadies to the sport, a tailwind provides the perfect environment. In a race situation, wind is a random element on which no plans can be made. On a training ride, however, the wind is central to the plan. When possible, Roadies will go to great lengths to plan their route so that the final miles of a ride take full advantage of a tailwind. It's viewed as a payoff. A Roadie earns the tailwind by fighting his way into the wind for many miles so that he can turn around and enjoy a boost.

Only in rare instances is it done in reverse. It never fails, though: Murphy's law of cycling requires that after a rider spends a few hours fighting a horrible headwind, the wind direction will change at the exact moment he reaches the turnaround point. That's bike racing!

Many coaches use a motorcycle to motorpace their rider at a speed he could never reach on his own. The coach rides the motorcycle at a speed of 35 to 40 mph while the rider follows closely behind, tucked in the draft. This is as close as one can get to replicating the speed and overall feeling of a bike race. It is a great training tool that helps elevate a rider's ability in a short time. Under close supervision with an experienced driver, this is a safe method of motorpace training.

There's another method that's not quite so safe. There is a brief but famous scene in the movie *Breaking Away* in which Dave is drafting a semi at speeds approaching 50 mph. Most Roadies are familiar with this scene and have attempted similar stunts. Some Roadies actively seek out this dangerous situation in an attempt to gain a good workout. They wait at an intersection that sees a high volume of truck traffic. When a truck stops at the intersection, it must slowly lumber its way back up to speed. In this time, a rider will position himself right behind the tailgate, where the draft is so powerful that it sucks him along. We call this dangerous activity "road surfing." Riders wait for the perfect truck to come by, much like a surfer waits for the perfect wave. They will ride the wave as long as they can and then drop off, circle back, and wait for the next truck.

The dangers of this tactic are too numerous to mention; I probably shouldn't even be writing about it. It's illegal in most states. The benefits are far outweighed by the risks. No one in the cycling world condones this type of riding. I don't endorse it. I only point it out as a demonstration of the lengths some riders will go to reach speeds unattainable in normal riding. Anyone who tries it is a scofflaw and a miscreant.

I only do it on Wednesday nights.

REACHING NIRVANA

Regardless of wind and barring an incident involving a motorist, a training ride can be a near-religious experience. Pushing your body to its limits can take you places most people don't know exist. Getting into a focused zone of total concentration can create a Zen-like state. It's a fascinating but purely selfish aspect of the sport. Even when it happens during a club ride, it's not something a rider can share with his riding companions. When it happens to more than one rider simultaneously, it is not acknowledged, and it can't be told in story form to a bystander. It doesn't benefit anyone but the rider who is experiencing it. And it is truly one of the strongest hooks of cycling.

At times, a training ride can take a rider beyond the point of a Zen-like state. But long before a Roadie reaches the point of mental exhaustion, he will have many more moments of clear thinking. It only makes sense. With all that blood coursing through the veins, the brain is provided with a constant flow of oxygen. That's a good thing. Many of the world's problems could be solved, puzzles answered, and theories formulated if people would just go for a long bike ride.

WHERE ELSE?

There's no other sport I know that sees this kind of dedication. I challenge you to name a sport that requires its participants to spend two to five hours alone a couple

Dude, WHERE'S MY BIKE?

After a long and very hard solo training ride at an area park, George peeled himself off his bike and leaned it against the back of his car. He slumped in the driver's seat and slowly changed out of his cycling shoes. He was completely wiped out after spending three hours hammering around the park.

He started the car, pulled away through the parking space, and drove the twenty-eight miles to his house. He then went inside and fixed himself something to eat. About an hour later, he went outside to feed his dog, and he saw his bike leaning against the side of his house.

"That's weird," he thought; "I don't remember leaving my bike there."

Indeed, he hadn't left his bike there. In his post-ride funk, he had left his $4,500 bike lying in the parking lot. Later a friend, Dave, noticed the bike and recognized it as George's. Dave drove twenty miles out of his way to deliver it to George's house. Not wanting to disturb George, he just leaned it against the house and left without making his presence known. Needless to say, George went through a period of great confusion as he tried to piece together the sequence of events.

This is a true story, and it shows a number of things about the cycling community. First, it shows that Roadies can identify each other by bike. It also shows that Roadies will go out of their way to reunite a rider with his bike. Most importantly, this shows us that a rider can put himself into such debt that he can lose some brain cells.

of times per week working at high output. It's nuts, yet it's something every Roadie must do if he wants to be competitive.

What's strange is that Roadies seldom recognize the fact that they're spending large chunks of time in total solitude. They focus on their objectives. They become completely absorbed in the task at hand. There are many people in this world who always need to be around other people. Roadies do not fall into this category. Conversely, there are many people in this world who would give their right arm for a chance to spend time alone. Roadies can't relate to that idea, either. This is not what we call "alone time." We call it "training."

If Roadies experience any regret for having chosen a sport of such abject solitude, it's when they ride past a backyard barbecue. Cars are parked up and down the street. The smell of the grill and the sound of laughter wafting out to the road conspire to remind a cyclist of just how alone he is.

We've all been there, and these are the only times we feel as though we're missing out on a normal life. But then again, we've been to many backyard barbecues where the conversation was painful, the food subpar, and lawn darts the only entertainment. On those occasions, as we look out to the road and notice a lone cyclist passing by, we feel envy that someone can be so completely free. The grass truly is greener on the other side of the fence.

FOUR SEASONS

Sometimes the grass isn't greener. Sometimes the leaves are browner. And the snow is whiter. Yes, the tone of these rides changes with the seasons. Training rides aren't limited to the summer months. Oh, no. Don't kid yourself.

Roadies feel an urgency to regain the fitness lost during the relative inactivity of winter, so they strive to get the greatest benefit out of every mile during the spring. The racing season is charging at them like a runaway train, and they are in a constant state of fear that their competition is riding more miles, working harder, becoming faster, and growing stronger. They fret that the miles they are riding are somehow inferior. They watch the bathroom scale for signs of fitness and obsess over the speed at which their fitness is returning. The miles are longer and most valued in the spring. Every minute on the bike means something.

In the summer, when they should be concentrating on their weaknesses, they will likely be working on their strengths. Many riders shy away from working on their weaknesses. For example, someone who is a great sprinter but a lousy climber will spend too much time working on his sprinting ability instead of his climbing ability. Why? He sprints because he likes doing it and he's good at it. It's human nature, and it's a trait that makes him a typical Roadie.

You may think that during racing season there should be fewer miles involved in training rides. I'll just warn you to not get too attached to this notion.

In the fall, the urgency is gone, but the habit remains. It is hard to find proper motivation, but since Roadies are used to spending so much time doing it, they get on the bike and try to sustain their fitness as long as they can before winter sets in. Many switch to a different bike in order to take a break from the routine. They may put knobby tires on their rain bike and ride it on dirt roads. They may segue right into the sport of cyclocross, which is an interesting mix of road cycling and mountain biking.

In the winter, Roadies resolve to train hard and keep their fitness all through the winter so that they'll be stronger in the spring. They may succeed. They may fail. Winter training rides, if you can get past the cold temperatures, snow, slush, and ice, can actually be quite nice. There's no pressure to stick to a rigid schedule. The racing season is at least three months away. These rides tend to be more thoughtful. It's a time when riders can take a step back, view the upcoming season from afar, and set their goals and objectives with a clear mind. The main concern is to prevent fitness from slipping away. A secondary concern is to keep the fingers and other extremities from freezing and falling off.

The other option is to ride on the rollers in the basement. Yuck!

THE EPIC

Every now and then, a Roadie will experience a ride that lasts longer than expected, goes farther than expected, and runs into more challenges than an ordinary ride.

We call these "epic rides." They are completely unplanned. To qualify as an epic ride, the training ride must contain some or all of the following elements:

- Being chased by a dog
- Being chased by a motorist
- Bonking
- Staying out long after sunset
- Getting rained on
- Getting snowed on
- Having the temperature change by 15 degrees
- Having a mechanical problem
- Getting horribly lost

A normal ride turns into an epic ride when a rider feels really good and decides to add miles. This decision may seem harmless, but it has turned out badly on more than one occasion. It's best to stick to the plan formulated at the start of the ride, when the brain was working at 100 percent capacity.

At some point in an epic ride, the objectives become less about training and more about survival. Oddly, a rider could end the battle by placing a call for help on the cell phone, but what fun would that be? Upon returning safely, a Roadie will be tempted to kiss the ground, though few actually do. It will become a topic for discussion for a while until it fades from memory. Eventually it will be replaced by another epic ride.

Ask any Roadie to tell you a story of an epic ride. I guarantee he will have several.

TOO MUCH OF A GOOD THING

It's not uncommon for Roadies to suffer from burnout as the season wears on. The bike becomes a ball and chain halfway through August. A sixty-mile training ride ends after the tenth mile due to lack of interest. Racing is still fun, but training becomes drudgery.

The key is to step away from the sport for a while or find a way to make a game of it. For example, I've developed the surf/golf/bike triathlon as a way to recharge my batteries. I haven't established a governing body yet, nor is this particular triathlon recognized by the International Olympic Committee, but I'll keep dreaming.

FINAL LAP

I can't overstate the importance of training rides. Without them, a bike racer is nothing more than an ordinary bike rider. Sure, a training ride requires a lot of time out of a Roadie's day. It requires a great amount of sacrifice. It chews into a bike racer's social life (or replaces it entirely). It requires as much effort as a race and sometimes more. It takes a lot out of a Roadie, leaving him to spend more time recovering. It serves a social purpose that is a key component of the activity.

Training rides are as much a part of the scene as the racing itself; in many cases, more so. The casual observer might wonder if Roadies train to race or if they race to give themselves something to train for.

All I know is, I don't train nearly enough. Ask any Roadie: He will say the same thing.

5. Nutrition and the Bonk

Nutrition is temporary. No matter how much we eat at a given meal, we will return to the table a few hours later. Most normal folk do this three times a day to consume the 1,500 to 2,000 calories necessary to function normally.

Roadies, of course, don't function normally. In one hour of intense riding, Roadies will burn an astounding 1,200 calories. In a three-hour race, that amounts to 3,600 calories. On a five-hour training ride, that's a staggering 6,000 calories. With the body burning calories at such a rate, nutrition becomes even more temporary. To keep up with their need for calories, Roadies consume food at regular intervals throughout the day and during the race. Most riders know precisely what they need to do to keep fuel in the tank. They count calories and grams with religious fervor. They eat a lot, and most are very particular about what they eat.

FEEDING A ROADIE

I was on a cycling road trip to Colorado with my teammates, and our hostess, Barb, insisted on making dinner for us. She asked the simple question, "What would you guys like for dinner?"

I, trying to be a low-maintenance guest, answered, "Anything's fine, Barb. We aren't too picky."

That couldn't have been further from the truth. The ensuing dialogue resembled lunchtime at a Weight Watchers meeting as every rider chimed in with his own list of dietary demands and restrictions. Eventually our gracious hostess threw up her hands and proclaimed that cyclists won't eat anything and therefore may starve to death. Fortunately, the situation wasn't as tense as it sounds, and Barb ended up fixing us the best plain noodles and chicken we had ever tasted. When she offered ice cream for dessert, I was the only one to accept. The other riders looked at me as if I had three noses.

"You're not going to eat that, are you?" George asked.

"Sure. Why not?" I responded.

"Do you have any idea what's in it?" he continued.

I answered with a blank stare. I am fully aware of what's in ice cream, and I'm also aware that few people die from eating it.

Some cyclists get hung up on their diet and refuse to put anything in their mouth that isn't on their approved list. Other cyclists, like me, believe that since they burn six zillion calories per hour when they ride, they can eat anything that resembles food. Every now and then it's okay to eat a double bacon-and-cheese quarter-pounder with extra grease. I wouldn't do it every night, but there are times in life when it's all that's available. Obviously the fuel that you put into an engine will determine the output. The adage "you are what you eat" is given a fair amount of weight in the cycling community.

All you need to know is that these dietary concerns can cause the rider to behave in an odd manner for no apparent reason, particularly in the hours leading up to a race. For example, do not be alarmed if you find a rider eating a bowl of granola at 6:00 p.m. It's up to him to know what's best for his body. If he wants to eat nothing but chicken and rice twenty-four hours a day, then all you can do is remind him of the importance of balance in a diet. And if you happen to be with him in a restaurant, do not be surprised when he orders a plain salad without dressing and then eats another bowl of cereal an hour later before bed. This is normal. Spaghetti for breakfast shouldn't surprise you either. After a ride, however, there are no limits to what a Roadie will eat. Stand back and allow plenty of room.

Simply put, each Roadie must learn all the angles of proper nutrition and then determine what works best for him. This includes the full range of dietary supplements such as ribose, L-glutamine, and leftover pizza. Learning which combination works best involves much research and trial and error. At the same time, a Roadie must be prepared to wing it. A fast-food drive-through window may be the only source of "nutrition" available.

ROLLING RESTAURANT

If a rider needs 6,000 calories for a five-hour ride, it's impossible to consume that much food prior to the ride. It would be physically impossible to get *on* the bike after a 6,000-calorie meal, let alone pedal it to the end of the driveway. Riders will ramp up their caloric intake in advance of a ride, but the bulk of the replenishing will take place while the ride is under way. The pockets on the back side of the jersey will be stuffed with all kinds of groceries.

In the old days, riders used to carry a banana and some Fig Newtons. In the 1990s, the sports nutrition industry experienced a boom when companies discovered that athletes would pay good money for energy bars that tasted a lot like cardboard sprinkled with wheat germ. Prior to 1990, these energy bars came in one flavor and were available only at bike shops, running shops, outdoor outfitters, and gyms. With the advent of flavor, energy bars gained enormous popularity and began appearing in a multitude of varieties at convenience stores, gas stations, golf pro shops, and truck stops.

There are also a million different sports drinks on the market. They are usually sold in powder form that Roadies mix into their water bottles before they get on the bike. The flavor has come a long way in recent years, but if the energy bars fall short of tasting like candy bars, then the sports drinks fall far short of tasting like Kool-Aid. And to be truthful, it doesn't matter what any of this stuff tastes like because it's not going to be eaten or sipped; it's going to be inhaled.

As with the solid foods, riders need some time to determine which product or combination of products works best for them. Once they make that determination, they stick to it with unwavering loyalty. It also becomes a part of the routine and ritual on race day. It usually takes a major influence to get them to make changes.

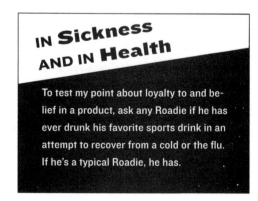

IN Sickness AND IN Health

To test my point about loyalty to and belief in a product, ask any Roadie if he has ever drunk his favorite sports drink in an attempt to recover from a cold or the flu. If he's a typical Roadie, he has.

FERMENTIA

An odd risk goes along with some of these Kool-Aid-type sports drinks. If a rider forgets to rinse his plastic water bottle after using it for a sports drink, the residual fluid will ferment. If neglected for more than a few days, the bottle will become a strange sort of science experiment, with spores. When this happens, there is almost no way to salvage the bottle. You'll never get the putrid smell out of it.

Eventually this fermentation will happen to a cyclist's favorite bottle: the one he bought at the bike shop in the faraway town while on vacation, or the one that some cycling superstar with an unpronounceable name threw away during a race. Be prepared to deal with this crisis.

Add water bottles to the list of cyclist-approved Christmas and birthday presents. They're cheap, and cyclists will always use them.

MEALS ON WHEELS

The feed zone and the way Roadies pick up their vittles during a long road race (see Chapter 13) need to be described. If you're not participating in the race, you may be recruited to perform feed-zone duties for someone who is. You will need to know something about it in advance.

Every rider will arrive at the race site with a cooler in his car packed with enough food to feed an army. Of course, since we're talking about cyclist food here, it's not something any army would care to eat. Sometime during the pre-race routine, each rider will set aside the food he wants to consume during the race. This food will then be placed in a musette bag. (Pronounce it however you like, but Roadies pronounce it myoo-ZET.) A musette bag is simply a cloth purse with a Velcro closure and a really long strap. In a typical musette, a rider will pack a handful of Fig Newtons, a banana, an energy bar, and a plastic bottle full of some sort of sports drink.

The Roadie will not take this bag with him into the race. Heavens, no! That would be too easy, and it would take all the fun out of the experience. Instead, he will give it to you. You will take it to the feed zone, where you will be joined by a hundred other loyal friends, siblings, and grandparents who have been recruited by their Roadies to help with these duties. You will wait for your Roadie to ride past at approximately 20 mph. You will stand at the edge of the road dangling the musette by its long strap. He will grab it as he swoops past, throw the strap around his head and arm so that the bag hangs open in front of him, and empty the contents into his jersey pockets. He will do this without slowing down! Moments later he will discard the empty musette bag farther up the road, where you will retrieve it and get it ready for the next feed zone.

Does that sound crazy? If there are 100 riders in the field and they're all trying to get musette bags handed to them at the same time, it will look like a dance scene out of *West Side Story*.

DEFINING THE FEED ZONE

The feed zone is a little like an aid station at a marathon run, but bigger and crazier. A feed zone is to an aid station what a grocery store is to a lemonade stand. It is a designated area on the racecourse where riders are permitted to take on more food and drink—the only place on the course where they are allowed to do so. They may carry as much as they wish, and they may eat and drink at any time, but they can only pick up additional supplies at these locations. The feed zone is usually about 200 meters long, demarcated with orange cones, and will likely be situated on an uphill section of road where riders will naturally be going more slowly. There will probably be a United States Cycling Federation official assigned to the feed zone to make sure everyone behaves properly.

One of the rules governing this area is that riders can pick up food only on the right side of the road. The widely accepted practice is for riders who are picking up food to move to the right and riders who have picked up their food to move to the left.

Imagine a busy expressway during rush hour. There's a lot of crisscrossing traffic, and there's always one guy who waits until the last minute to jump across four lanes of traffic to get to his exit. In the feed zone, that's normal.

The feed zone is usually located at the twenty-five- or thirty-mile point of a race and at regular intervals thereafter. Depending on the length of the race, there may be four or five feed zones. Riders are responsible for making their own arrangements to get their food to each feed zone as well as to have it handed to them. That means they're also responsible for making sure they can find their food and the person who is holding it when the time comes. Remember that there will be 100 others trying to do the same thing.

Ask any Roadie to tell you of his surefire methods for finding his feeder.

WHO ORDERED THE VEGETARIAN?

Most riders will give detailed instructions on what they would like to have handed to them at certain points during a race.

"Okay, here's the plan. At the first feed, I'll want one PowerBar, one bottle of water, two Fig Newtons, and one banana," he tells his willing helper. And that's exactly what the helper carefully packs into the musette.

In the heat of battle, however, a rider will forget what he asked for and demand something else as he flies through the feed zone in a panic.

"Just give me a Coke and some Oreos! Nothing else!" he'll yell as he passes at 25 mph using a tone of voice that says, "For chrissakes, what is wrong with you? Can't you read my mind?"

Coke and Oreos? What? But he said Fig Newtons and a banana!

Of course, he never said to pack Oreos, nor did he specify whether he wanted Double Stuf Oreos, reduced-fat Oreos, or regular Oreos. Did he want the generic brand that looks like Oreos but isn't from Nabisco? Who knows? At no time during the pre-race preparations did he mention anything about a can of Coke. Not once did he ask for Cherry Coke, Diet Coke, Vanilla Coke, regular Coke, Coke Zero, or a generic equivalent. The lesson here? It's best to let the rider pack the cooler and thus take ownership of the situation.

REMEMBER TO LET GO

Ask any Roadie to tell you the story of the well-meaning friend who yanked the rider off his bike as he passed through the feed zone because he forgot to let go of the musette. Don't let this happen to you. Insist on practicing the art of the "hand-up" in the privacy of your driveway. Ten minutes spent working on this important skill will be time well spent.

When a car runs out of fuel, it will coast to a stop. When a Roadie runs out of fuel, his race is over. I can't stress the importance of getting the food into the Roadie's hands. However, there's no guarantee he'll remember to eat it.

I know that sounds impossible, but it's absolutely true. After all the trouble you went through to get the food into his hands, he can forget to eat it. Granted, sometimes he forgets to take sufficient quantities along with him, but sometimes, in the heat of battle, there may not be a convenient time to eat; riders may concentrate so hard on tactics and countertactics that they completely overlook nutrition. Moreover, in this situation, the need to eat and drink isn't based on hunger and thirst but on the body's need for energy: If riders wait until they're hungry or thirsty, it's usually too late.

The human body reacts to this neglect. We call it "the Bonk." The first time I ever heard someone mention the Bonk, I had no idea what he was talking about. I thought it was a sound the bike makes.

It's not a sound. It's a feeling.

OH, WHAT A FEELING!

Here is the technical explanation. When Roadies ride hard, they deplete their liver glycogen stores, and the liver releases insufficient amounts of sugar into the bloodstream. Riders may have plenty of muscle glycogen, but without the liver glycogen helping to supply the brain with a steady blood-sugar level, they will feel lightheaded, uncoordinated, and, most problematic, weak.

The Bonk is a bizarre occurrence that puts the body through an amazing array of feelings that every rider should try to avoid. It's a feeling of weakness and malaise that permeates every single muscle. The Bonk manifests itself in different ways for different people. The adjectives I heard most often when asking Roadies to describe the feeling are "spongy," "hollow," and "tingly." One rider said his legs change from iron to pulp. Interesting. It's not exhaustion, nor is it sore legs. Those are defeating, but they're nothing like the hit-by-a-truck feeling of the Bonk.

For me, the first uh-oh feeling comes after about two and a half hours of hard riding. By the time I feel the first knock, I'm already behind the game. If I eat something immediately, I can lessen the severity of the Bonk, but I won't regain full power for several hours. If no food is available, the strange spongy feeling will set in just a few miles later, and I will start to unravel. At this point, it's as if someone has pulled the little rubber stopper out of the drain, and all remaining energy has spiraled down the tube (counterclockwise in the Southern Hemisphere). My body feels limp and shapeless, yet I must continue to ride because I have to make it home.

When I'm deep in the throes of the Bonk, my bike manages to stay upright only because the front wheel acts as a stabilizing gyro. My bike manages to keep moving

because I've shut down all other bodily functions to direct all of my energy into the act of pedaling. I am impervious to potholes and bumps. I feel no temperature. Wind and the elements are the least of my concerns. I can look only at the road ahead of me and nothing else. I count the miles that remain between me and home. From previous bouts of the Bonk, I already know the shortest and flattest route back to my house. For some odd reason, I also tend to get sleepy. I'm a zombie on wheels.

TAKING FOOD ON THE RUN

In the throes of the Bonk, desperate for something to eat, I've taken food from total strangers along the road: tomatoes from a roadside vegetable stand, apples from a front-yard apple tree, and dinner rolls from a stranger's plate at a sidewalk café. The ability to pilfer food is a survival technique that Roadies develop early in their cycling life. When the Bonk settles in, food is the only thing that will help.

George once Bonked so badly during a training ride that he had to send his friend ahead to find food and bring it back to him. Neither of them had food in his pocket, so the loyal servant had to ride up the road while George ambled along at a blistering pace of 5 mph. That was all he could muster when the Bonk Monster attacked.

During a Bonkfest, Roadies will be forced to temporarily suspend their strict food regimen. It may be the only time you ever see a Roadie devour a full sleeve of Thin Mints Girl Scout cookies (wrapper and all). Beggars can't be choosers, nor can they curl up and sleep on the shoulder of the road.

The Bonk occurs more often during a training ride than in a race situation. Roadies usually learn their lesson and take precautions to prevent it from happening during a race. A lengthy road race offers more opportunity to deplete the energy stores. It probably won't happen in a criterium or a time trial because the duration is seldom more than sixty minutes. Each rider comes to know his body well enough to know what he needs to eat and when he needs to eat it. I pity the rider who makes the mistake on the day of a race. The day, I can assure you, will be ruined.

If a rider misses his opportunity to eat during a road race due to a botched hand-up at a feed zone, he may find himself in a world of hurt later in the race. This is why it's important for him to practice the hand-up with his support crew so they don't drop the food when the heat is on. Come crunch time, you will need to perform this ballet without fail. Any amount of practicing that two people can do will increase their chances for success.

FINAL LAP

The Bonk happens to every Roadie at least once. Each time he vows to never let it happen again. But it does. He can take solace in knowing that even the best riders Bonk. Ask Lance Armstrong. He once missed a feed during a mountain stage of the Tour de France, Bonked badly, and nearly lost it. I'll leave that and other stories of survival to the Roadies of the world to tell.

Should a Roadie suffer a Bonk or any other travesty, it's his teammates who work overtime to keep him in the race. Even Lance Armstrong needed his teammates.

PART TWO
CLASSROOM SESSIONS

6. Drafting and the Breakaway

I've waited until now to lay a rather startling fact on you: Bike racing is a team sport. Make no mistake about it. Though most people think of it as an individual activity, it is quite possibly the ultimate team sport. In the coming chapters, I will explain some team tactics and how they affect races. For now, just accept this as truth: Cycling is a club-based activity but a team-based sport. It will be my job to convince you.

While it is perfectly acceptable for an individual rider to participate in a bike race independently, a team has a better chance of producing top results.

Cycling teams are not limited in the number of members on their roster, nor are they limited in the number of riders who may participate in any given event. On one weekend you may have seven teammates show up for a race, and on the next weekend you may have three teammates show up. Whatever your team allows, the sport allows.

EVERYONE PLAYS

When I played Little League baseball, our coach would wait until we had a 30-run lead before allowing the weaker players to play. If you missed a practice, you weren't allowed to play at all. Eventually rules were created to ensure that everyone played a certain number of innings in a game. It was a part of the politically correct movement of the 1990s to remove all evidence of competition from sports. Everyone's a winner; there are no losers.

In bike racing, there is no need for such a rule. You simply sign up to race, and then you race. There is no bench for you to sit on. There are no mandatory practices. It's simple: If you're not prepared, you'll get dropped. The pack will ride away from you, and you'll have no one to blame for your lack of preparation. On the other hand, if you go through the necessary preparation, you will contribute to your team's success and share in the victory.

A team's objectives are relatively simple: Objective 1 is to get someone from your team across the finish line first. Objective 2 is to get as many of your teammates as you can—including yourself—in the top 10. Objective 3 is to have fun. It's a bike race! Let the good times roll.

How you achieve those objectives is up to your team to decide. I'll provide some examples of team tactics in this chapter.

PUNCHING A HOLE IN THE WIND

The first thing you simply must know about cycling tactics is that drafting plays a role in everything that happens in a bike race. In the motor-sports world of NASCAR, they make a big hairy huzzah about drafting. That's where most casual sports fans first learn of the concept. Folks, I'm here to tell you that drafting in a NASCAR race doesn't come close to the importance of drafting in cycling. Drafting is to cycling what sugar is to candy. It is a key component to everything that happens in a bike race.

The draft is nothing more than the absence of wind. It is a pocket of calm air. A low-pressure center. How this phenomenon works and how it affects a bike race are a bit complex, and since nobody wants to revisit ninth grade science class, I promise not to use too much scientific drivel in my explanation. Instead, I like to use the following model. Follow me . . . literally.

ON RAMP

Imagine that you're driving in a very small car, and you're entering a freeway via an entrance ramp. For the sake of realism, let's pretend it's partly cloudy with no wind. You have a full tank of gas.

The road is empty except for you and a very large truck in front of you. The truck is fully loaded, which makes it slow to accelerate. As a result, you'll be right up close to its bumper. Stay there. Avoid the temptation to zoom out into the left lane. This explanation falls apart if you pass the truck. Stay close to the truck's rear bumper even though it's unsafe and against the law; this is only an example. In cycling, we describe this position as being "on a wheel" or "in the draft."

At a speed of 20 mph, neither you nor the truck would feel any effect of a headwind because there isn't much. To prove this, you can pull out from behind the truck and easily maintain your speed with no trouble at all. You could even pass the truck with no trouble, but instead, stay there and make note of the fact that there is hardly any headwind at 20 mph. As a result, there is little effect of a draft.

At 40 mph, your small car will do fine as you stay behind the truck. There is no wind turbulence for you to fight because the truck is punching a big hole in the wind, and you're sitting comfortably in the draft. You're also getting good gas mileage. To test this, move out from behind the truck. Your engine's RPMs will go up a little. It would be easy to maintain pace with the steadily moving truck, but your fuel wouldn't last as long.

At 60 mph, you can cruise along nicely behind the truck. If you try to pull out from behind the truck into the next lane, the wind will slow you down a little. Your RPMs will rise sharply. You'll burn gas quickly. This is a good cruising speed, but it's not easy to maintain on your own for very long.

At 80 mph, you may find the speed rather intoxicating. You might get ambitious and foolishly try to pass the truck. As you attempt this, your car will bog down under the strain of pushing all the air, and you will burn fuel much faster. Your RPMs may not go into the danger zone right away, but they will after a short time. Immediately, when you return to the draft behind the truck, your RPMs will drop back down as if turning off a switch. Remember that it's a calm day. Any headwind you perceive is actually being created by your own speed.

At 100 mph, the idea of passing the truck is preposterous. You already have your gas pedal mashed against the floorboard, and your tiny car is doing everything it can just to hold on to the draft. It is critical to know exactly where the draft is. If any part of your car gets out of the draft, you will begin to lose speed. If you decide to move out from behind the truck now, the wind will cause you to lose ground.

As that gap grows, you'll soon find yourself out of the draft altogether and catching 100 percent of the wind. You can maintain 100 mph on your own, but you will burn all of your gas in a short time. You may buy some time if you take steps to become more aerodynamic. Reach out and rip off your side mirrors, windshield wipers, and radio antenna. Put tape over your door handles. You should have washed and waxed your car because the dirt isn't helping your aerodynamics.

Earlier in the day, you laughed at a cyclist wearing the tight-fitting jersey and Lycra tights, but now you understand. Anything that tickles the wind is hurting your speed, and it is magnified at high speeds.

You realize, of course, that the speeds I've used in my example are much different on a bike, right? No way are we ever going to reach speeds of 60, 80, and 100 mph, but they translate to percentages pretty well. For example, a Roadie can ride all day at 20 percent and 40 percent. However, at 100 percent, a Roadie is only going to last a few moments.

DIFFERENT EFFECTS

That truck has a bigger engine and a bigger gas tank. Your car is weaker and has a smaller tank. For you to match speed with a stronger truck requires an equalizing factor: the draft. It allows you to go as fast without using the same amount of energy.

Had you been driving an identical truck with an identical engine and an identical gas tank, what would have happened? How would the draft have affected the scenario? That's simple. The truck on the front was pushing more air, which means it was using more energy to travel the same speed as you, which means it would run out of gas before your truck.

The critical thing to remember is that the drafter/follower is working approximately 30 percent less than the draftee/leader. Obviously, when the speed increases, the need to be tucked into the draft is greater. Riders who don't buy into this idea will have a tough time in a bike race.

WHERE'S THE DRAFT?

Just because you're directly behind the truck doesn't guarantee you'll feel the benefits of the draft. The location of the draft will change depending on the direction of the wind, strength of the wind, speed of the truck, and direction the truck is traveling in relation to the wind direction. At risk of overstating the obvious, if the wind is coming from the left, then the draft will be located slightly to the right. And vice versa. If you listen to the wind noise around your windows, it will tell you where the wind is. Your goal should be to tuck your car into the wind shadow.

Amazingly, some Roadies never fully grasp this concept. While everyone else is forming into an echelon to get out of the wind, some Roadies will remain in a straight line. They think they're in the draft, but they're actually catching a face full of wind and therefore are working harder than necessary to maintain the same speed.

It's important for a cyclist to understand how the draft works to enjoy any success in this sport. It is central to every tactic and strategy.

So, now that you have a better understanding of the concept of drafting, let's get back on the expressway and play around with the model.

FIVE-CAR STUD

We now know that your car has the ability to drive at 100 percent speed for a moment or two without the help of the truck's draft, but you will need to rest the engine soon or it will blow a gasket.

In our current example, the truck is removed. You are now the leader, and you have four identical cars lined up bumper to bumper behind you, tucked into your draft at 100 mph. You are in the number-one spot, or as we say, "on the front." This follow-the-leader formation is called a paceline. Now we're going to get fancy with it.

Twenty seconds of this 100 percent effort will cause your engine's warning light to come on. Because you don't want to explode, you pull into the left lane, slow down a little, and allow the four other cars to pass you. When you let up on the gas and slow down, your warning light goes out. That's a relief!

When all four cars pass you, you hop back into line in the number-five spot. We refer to this as being "on the back." You're now in the draft again and working 30 percent less. You're still going 100 mph, but it's not as painful. This gives your engine a chance to cool down.

One at a time, each of the four cars takes a turn at the front for a few seconds before moving aside and rotating to the back of the line. Soon you find yourself "on the front" again. Repeat this process over and over. This is called a rotating paceline. (This can be done with any number of cyclists in a single-file line or two abreast.)

DO THE MATH

See what's happening here? You'll be working hard (100 percent) when you're on the front, and you'll be resting (70 percent) when you're drafting behind the other four cars. That's a 4-to-1 ratio of rest to work. As a result, you're able to work at 70 percent output for 80 percent of the time. With that built-in rest period, you'll find that you're able to go 100 percent for a longer period when it's your turn on the front. This means that you're able to go faster as a group than you would be able to alone.

The sum of everyone's effort is greater than the amount of their individual capabilities. Please read that line again. It's a gem. We've just defined synergy better than any other sport can define it.

The rotating thing is very cool. You will help this five-person rotating paceline maintain its top speed while working at your max for 20 percent of the time. In other words, if you stay in the draft, you will work up to 30 percent less than the rider ahead of you who has his nose in the wind. Even though it's just an approximation, 30 percent is a lot. And the ability to use just 70 percent of one's energy allows a rider to rest and recover. During a bike race, this little rest period is as close as a cyclist gets to sitting on the bench. By contrast, during a football game more than half the team sits on the bench for minutes at a time.

Now the terminology makes more sense. The schmuck who is riding "on the front" is said to be "pulling" or "taking a pull" because it feels like he's pulling everyone along. Those behind him are said to be "sitting in" because they're sitting in the draft. (If you "sit in" too much, people will call you a "wheel sucker," and they won't mean it in a nice way.)

Roadies know how important it is to spend and save energy wisely. Every rider enters the race with a finite amount of energy. Spending it wisely is critical; saving it for when it's really needed is the key to success. Many inexperienced riders, in

DOES IT REALLY PULL?

Let me supply an example of the pulling effect.

Take your car for a drive on the open road. Roll down the window and stick your hand outside. Play with the air currents that are rushing past your window. Hold your arm still and move your hand in different directions and see how this affects the tug of the wind. Turn the palm of your hand directly toward the wind so that you are catching a handful of air and hold for a couple of minutes.

Next, slowly move your hand to a spot directly behind the side mirror so that it's protected from the wind. As you do this, it will almost feel like the mirror is pulling your hand like a magnet. It is, in fact, your arm that's feeling less resistance as your hand moves forward. But since it feels like the mirror is pulling the hand forward, we refer to this "pull" as something tangible.

Just to protect myself, I'm going to insist that you let someone else drive the car while you conduct this experiment. I don't want anyone to get in an accident. Also, be sure that you're using the side mirrors for this experiment and not the mirror that's inside the car. That's critical to the success of the demonstration.

addition to having trouble finding the draft, haven't developed the ability to throttle back 30 percent once they do find it. They burn a lot of extra energy when they're in the rest/recovery position of a paceline because they don't know which muscles to rest. They haven't learned how to gauge their output. This will come back to haunt them later in the race when they call upon energy reserves that are no longer there.

Experienced riders, on the other hand, know exactly how much energy they need to expend to keep up with a paceline. They can turn it on and off like a switch. They know the importance of conserving energy, so they know how to actively rest certain muscle groups and thus save valuable energy for more crucial points in the race.

THE DRAFT-O-METER

How does this drafting and paceline stuff apply to a bike race? Drafting is a device that riders use to conserve their energy. A paceline is the smart use of drafting to maintain higher speeds. A bike race is a constantly changing equation. Riders are constantly reassessing and recalculating the following components:

- Output
- Distance to the finish line
- Opponents' strength
- Speed of the race
- Terrain
- Wind direction
- Personal energy reserves

Obviously the only component over which riders have any control is their own output. The draft and paceline are tools to help conserve their output.

This is why we place so much importance on drafting and how it's used in strategies. Roadies are constantly trying to find the perfect balance between drafting/resting and attacking/working.

The Draft in Action

Question: Once a bike race starts, where do you suppose most Roadies want to be positioned? On the front? Or sitting in?

Answer: They want to be near the front but don't want to be the lead rider. Why? Because they want to be protected from the wind. They want to have at least one rider in front of them to punch a hole in the wind, so they can save their energy.

On or At

A Roadie will say "on the front" when referring to the front-most rider, the one pushing the wind. Roadies will say "at the front" when referring to any position in the first few rows of riders.

Think of it in terms of a soldier in battle during the Civil War. Let's say Private Huber is sent from Washington to deliver a message to Colonel Phinney at Gettysburg. Private Huber will not find the colonel on the front line shooting at Confederate soldiers. Instead, Colonel Phinney will be sitting on a horse well behind the lines but within sight of his troops. He is "at the front" and has a 70 percent chance of getting shot, while his troops are "on the front" and have a 100 percent chance of taking a bullet for the cause.

The front part of the race is where the racing takes place. It's where the attacks happen. Anyone who is going to establish a lead is going to do it from the front. (Anyone who attempts to establish a lead by going "off the back" will never enjoy success in this arena.) Obviously, not everyone can be on/at the front of a field containing 100 riders on a road that's twenty-two feet wide, so riders at the front wage a constant battle to hold their position. It's the constant battle to be at the front that drives the speed of the race.

So your next questions may be, Why do riders attack? When do they decide to attack? How do team tactics play into an attack?

PLAYING THE NUMBERS GAME

Here's some simple math for you to consider. With 100 riders in the field, the odds of winning the race are 99 to 1. (Keep in mind there is no limit to how many riders can enter a given race. I like to use the number 100 for this example because it's a nice round number, and I'm not too good at math. I don't want to lead anyone astray by implying that there is a limit to the size of the field.)

Odds of 99 to 1 aren't so great, are they? They're better than playing the lottery, but they still stink. Faced with those horrible odds, any rider who wants to win the race should have the same thought: Improve the odds of winning the race. One good way to do this is by reducing the number of competitors. If this were an episode of *Murder, She Wrote,* we could come up with several diabolical ways to do away with our competitors. Instead, we'll have to use the most basic race tactic: the breakaway.

A breakaway is simply the act of leaving the rest of the riders behind before the end of the race. A single rider can do it alone. Two riders can do it together. A group of twenty riders can make it happen. It can be done with any combination of riders from any combination of teams. And here is the one astounding thing that sets bicycle racing apart from all other sports: Members of two or more teams might work together toward this common goal.

Think about that for a moment: competitors in cahoots. How bizarre is that? Would you *ever* see two opponents working together in football? Never. Baseball? Basketball? Hockey? Soccer? Competitive knitting? Forget it. It's not going to happen.

THE ATTACK OF THE KILLER ROADIES

A breakaway usually begins when a rider attacks the field by sprinting ahead and establishing a lead. He may do this according to his team's game plan, or he may attack on impulse when an opportunity crops up. There are no rules that govern this. The lead may be as little as ten or fifteen meters. If the field is slow to respond, then it may be more. There is no set distance for this. It's purely arbitrary.

So let's imagine that our teammate George has attacked and is now riding alone out in front of the field with a slight lead of fifty meters. It's unlikely that he intends to ride away from everyone. He is one man against a hundred. Though every rider dreams of doing so, few riders have the ability to simply ride away from the field.

GAPS AND BRIDGES

When George establishes a gap between himself and the field, riders from other teams will react by trying to jump across that gap to connect with George. If they can catch George, they'll have a chance to get a breakaway started.

To keep it simple, let's assume that only two riders were able to jump away from the field and bridge the gap to George.

Suddenly, instantaneously, without uttering a word, these three riders must form an efficient rotating paceline. They will need to quickly get that synergy working in order to maximize their speed. They cannot take the time to discuss their chances. There is no time for polite introductions. There is time to do only one thing: work. Behind them, ninety-seven riders are gunning for them. The field is the horse, and these three riders are the carrot that is dangling in front of the horse's face.

FOUR FRONTS

With a breakaway established off the front, we have five distinct activities happening at once.

1. We have three riders from different teams attempting to get synergy working for them so they can ride away from the field.
2. We have riders who will try to jump across the gap to join the breakaway.
3. We have riders who are trying to block any chase effort.
4. We have riders who will be trying to bring it all back together by chasing down the escapees.
5. Let's not forget the riders who are just trying to stay with the field and finish the race. They are referred to as field fodder, and they have little impact on the race. I mention them here because despite being field fodder, they still work much harder than athletes in other sports. (Besides, that's where you'd find me!)

Let's look at the first four activities separately. Pay attention; this is good stuff, but it gets complicated.

Operation 1: Cooperation

For the breakaway riders, the race will be somewhat boring. They will simply ride as hard as they can until they are caught by the field or until they cross the finish line. Their freedom may last for thirty seconds or for the rest of the race. It may last for three seconds. It all depends on the other three operations.

The breakaway riders will quickly form their own cooperative group. By working together as opponents, they will break all the conventional rules of sport. I can't stress this bizarre occurrence enough. The idea of working with your enemy is absurd.

Operation 2: Chasing and Joining

These riders are only interested in joining the breakaway. They're convinced that the breakaway will succeed and they want to be a part of it. So they attack the field like lightning at a time when the gap in front of them can still be crossed. They try to create a gap behind them while closing the gap in front of them. In other words, they try to make a clean break of things and get across that gap with economy of motion.

With their noses in the wind, they'll be making 100 percent effort. Consequently, they will try to time their attack accordingly and not bite off more than they can chew. It really stinks to run out of gas half-way across the gap.

Operation 3: Minding the Gap

The breakaway has three riders, each one from a different team. Therefore, we should see members from those same three teams riding at the front of the field acting as sheepdogs to hold the group together and prevent other riders from chasing down the leaders. (I'll tell you how they do this in a moment.) This blocking tactic allows their teammate to escape from the field, thus improving their team's odds of winning to 3 to 1. That's a lot better than 99 to 1.

If I've made blocking sound easy, I've misled you. Blocking requires constant vigilance. It also requires constant reaction to counterattacks from the opposition. These countermeasures require great physical effort and provide few opportunities to rest and recover from each effort. It is a complete sacrifice of our own desire to do well in the race. We're giving up a lot to ensure the success of our teammate.

The commonly held belief is that in return for our efforts as Guardians of the Gap, the team will share the victory and all the spoils that go with it. We pin our hopes on George winning the race and then taking us out to dinner to celebrate afterward at the restaurant of our choice. And I'm ordering the most expensive entrée on the menu.

Blocking happens in two basic ways. The most obvious way to block the field is to go to the front and slow down. This causes the riders behind you to slow down as well. However, this method isn't as easy as it sounds, and it's only effective in certain situations.

The other way to block the field is a little more passive. It involves disrupting the rhythm of the chase. Here's how it's done. Let's pretend that our teammate, George, is in a breakaway that holds a fifty-second lead. Accordingly, it becomes our responsibility to protect the gap.

Suddenly an ambitious rider attacks the field and attempts to bridge the gap. We react swiftly by sprinting to get on his wheel and in his draft. Once there, we will wait.

Making A CLEAN BREAK

The riders who are chasing the breakaway can be compared to people who, after graduating from high school, stop consorting with their mundane high school friends when they realize that their new college friends are more hip. They feel the need to make a clean break from the friends of the past in order to join the friends of the future.

It won't be long before he looks over his shoulder. He does this expecting and hoping to see someone who is willing to continue what he has started, someone who is willing to pull through, assume the lead, rotate through a paceline, and continue at the same pace.

Instead, he will see us. We are unwilling to help him chase the breakaway because George is in it. We will demonstrate our unwillingness by slowing down. He will be disappointed. Even though he was able to reduce the gap by five seconds, our efforts will help regain those seconds and add more.

We will continue to do this every time someone attempts to pick up the pace. By defeating their rhythm, we will make it nearly impossible for them to sustain a high speed.

As blockers, we ride near the front of the field and remain vigilant as we watch for and react to anyone who attacks. This means that we must repeatedly accelerate to meet any challenger. Ask any Roadie which task is more difficult: riding in the breakaway or blocking the chase.

Operation 4: Reel Time

This group is interested not in joining the breakaway but in closing the gap and preventing the breakaway from succeeding. There are a couple of reasons for doing this.

Reason 1: Perhaps their team is not represented in the breakaway. Efforts to bridge across to it have failed, so riders simply want to reel it in like a mackerel so that they can reshuffle the deck. Therefore, they increase their speed to catch the leaders.

FINDING the RIGHT MIX

Question I: Would we want George to be in a four-man breakaway with Superman, Popeye, and Steve Austin—the Six Million Dollar Man?

Answer: Probably not. Those guys are strong enough to escape from the peloton, but George would have no chance of beating any of them in the final sprint. Especially Superman; that guy can sprint!

Question 2: Would we want George to be in a four-man breakaway with Regis Philbin, Jackie Chan, and Vanna White?

Answer: Probably not. Oh sure, he could whip them in the final sprint, but they don't seem like they'd have the strength to stay away. They lack chemistry. They aren't really powerful. It's not a good mix.

Question 3: What's the best mix?

Answer: The ideal scenario is to have George in a breakaway with riders who have the strength/chemistry/wherewithal to ride away from the field, but riders we know George can beat in the final sprint. This is a determination that we need to make as soon as a breakaway group is formed. With it, we will decide whether to protect the gap or reel the whole thing in and try again.

Reason 2: Perhaps the team has a fast sprinter with a racehorse mentality. It prefers to have the field remain together so that it can beat everyone with the sprint.

Reason 3: George is representing our team in the breakaway, but George may not be our strongest rider. Perhaps we don't feel confident that George is suited for the task. Or perhaps we know that his two breakaway companions aren't strong enough to carry it to victory. It's a hopeless cause, so we must initiate an effort to reel it back in.

OFF THE FRONT AND UP THE ROAD

Now is a good time for me to give you some terminology that you can use when talking about breakaways. "Off the front" is a popular expression that refers to anything that has a lead over the field. For example, if George attacks the field and establishes a small gap, he is said to be "off the front."

Being off the front differs from being up the road. When a breakaway goes "up the road," the riders are out of reach and only a heroic effort will catch them.

Is the race over when a breakaway goes up the road? Never! The race is never over until someone's front tire crosses the finish line. Many a breakaway has been caught within sight of the finish line.

This happens often in this crazy sport and is one of the reasons why bike races are exciting right up to the end. Though a breakaway may appear to have the race well in hand, it really ain't over till it's over.

FRIEND OR FOE?

At some point during their escape, riders in a breakaway will look around at their breakaway companions, size them up, and decide if they like their own personal chances for success. Just because they've improved their odds mathematically doesn't negate the fact that they still have to beat their breakaway companions to the finish line. The sooner they realize this, the better. As I mentioned before, it does a racer no good to be the weakest rider in a breakaway if he knows in advance that he can't beat anyone in the final sprint.

IT ALL LOOKS THE SAME TO ME

Is it possible for a spectator to go to a bike race and see what I've described in this chapter? Sometimes yes, sometimes no.

Things can get confusing when multiple breakaways form. For one thing, there's no limit to the size of a breakaway. It can be two riders or fifteen riders. Conversely, small chase groups may form between the breakaway and the field. There is no limit to the size of a chase group.

There is also no limit to the number of chase groups. If the breakaway has a two-minute lead over the field, there may be two, three, or four chase groups in that two-minute gap, all of whom have broken free of the field and are making their way across the gap attempting to join the leaders. You may see the peloton unravel into several small groups until there is nothing left of it.

IN THE BLINK OF AN EYE

All of the scenarios mentioned in this chapter may take place several times during the course of a race. They may happen simultaneously. They may happen in a million variations. They happen quickly. Everything I just described may happen three or four times in the span of a kilometer! The maneuvers can happen so fast that they are impossible to recognize.

Getting a breakaway started is never automatic. It can happen on the first try, or it can take several tries. It may not happen at all.

A more difficult task for spectators is to differentiate between one rider and the next. Quite frankly, they all look alike. Though each team wears a distinctive jersey, the entire field blends into one big blur of color. It's nearly impossible to tell them apart. The ability to detect tactics, then, depends on the ability to know who's who. That comes with time.

A seasoned cycling spectator can differentiate riders at a glance based on subtle things such as their pedaling motion or the way they sit on the bike. You will soon be able to tell if a rider is struggling by his posture, or how fresh a rider is by the expression on his face. Until then, though, it can be difficult to tell that the riders even have faces.

Part of the excitement of watching a bike race or participating in one is in knowing that riders are constantly working to initiate a breakaway. It's never just a bunch of guys riding around in circles really fast; each attack consists of a rider who hopes to win the race by taking a chance and trying to make something happen. Each attack is an attempt by contenders to separate themselves from the also-rans.

FINAL LAP

The breakaway is a great way to achieve success. But it's not the only way.

7. The Sprint, the Solo, the Combine, and Others

Please bear with me if I state the obvious. A sprint is a short, well-timed explosion of speed used to beat other riders to a certain point such as a finish line. It's a matter of having not simply the highest top-end speed but a combination of speed and timing. It's a furious amalgamation of strength, quickness, fearlessness, and ego.

Physically, it involves getting your butt off the saddle and pulling the handlebars in a fashion that leverages more force into the pedals. It is a visually dynamic image, particularly when there are several cyclists doing it at once in close proximity. It looks dangerous. It is flashy and fast and the favorite part of the sport for spectators and Roadies alike.

It is an ability that isn't bestowed on every rider. It involves fast-twitch muscles and strong resolve—things not every Roadie possesses. Some Roadies are really good at it. Some Roadies aren't.

DON'T BLINK

Imagine the racers have been out for four hours, racing unseen strategies on unseen roads. Finally they approach the finish line, where we've been standing and waiting all day, killing time reading magazines, making small talk, and eating stale bagels. Now picture this huge pack of 100 riders barreling down the two-lane road gunning for the finish line. Scary, sure, but also one of the most exciting, beautiful sights in the entire sporting world. As you stand in awe, please remember that since no breakaway formed in this race, the odds of winning are 99 to 1. It's the well-timed, fearless speedsters who have the best chance of winning. If you're not a good sprinter, your odds are on the weak side of 99 to 1.

The sprint happens fast. Ten to fifteen seconds is the average viewing time from the moment the riders come into view until the instant they pass the finish line. Just like that, it's over! What? We waited four hours for this? What's all this talk about cycling being a "rolling chess game"? It looks like a chaotic blur.

The "rolling chess game" took place throughout the race. The sprint is the final move of that chess game. If we were to watch the race in slow motion, we would see the teamwork taking place among the melee.

RED, GREEN, AND BLUE

To examine what is happening, let's create an example that includes two of our friends, George and Larry, riding on a fictitious team. We'll dress them in red so that they're easy to spot in our minds. We'll also place a blue team and a green team in this scenario, but we want the red team to win.

In the sprint I just mentioned, our red teammates seemed to sprint independently of one another, giving no thought to the team. Somehow, the fact that they're all wearing identical jerseys was lost on them. As such, working by himself for himself, neither George nor Larry could beat the 99-to-1 odds. George was in sixth place, Larry in tenth.

Many teams would be ecstatic with that result, but we're not satisfied; we want to win. Consequently, we'll have to devise a better plan. At the next race, we will utilize all of our red teammates to employ a different tactic: the lead-out. And since Larry admits that he is not a great sprinter, we're going to sacrifice Larry to set up our team's best sprinter: George.

AIR-TO-SURFACE MISSILE

If you were a fighter pilot on a mission to launch an air-to-surface missile at a target that's ten miles away, would you pull the trigger and fire the missile just as soon as you leave the runway? No, of course not. The missile would run out of fuel and fall short of the target. Instead, you would carry the missile as close as possible to the target to make sure it will actually reach the target.

That's what we're going to do. We will have Larry provide George an escort. Larry's sole responsibility will be to keep the pace high and allow George to sit in his draft and carry the same speed without expending 100 percent energy.

When George thinks he's close enough and can make it to the target on his own, he will launch his sprint. This is where timing plays an important role. If George leaves the draft too soon, he will run out of steam. If he waits too long, other sprinters may beat him to the punch.

At the next race, when we replay the scene of 100 riders coming down the road gunning for the finish line, we know one of the tactics being used: George is following his escort, Larry.

Again, this tactic is called a lead-out. Larry is leading George to the finish line. It puts George in a great position to unleash his sprint. He's near the front and has a reliable wheel to follow to the finish line, yet he's working 30 percent less. If George times it right, he will beat the other sprinters. Brilliant, yes?

Well, to be honest, it could be more brilliant. For one thing, it's probably too much to ask Larry to set that fast pace by himself. If we have more teammates in the race, then we should put them to work during the last mile.

ALL ABOARD!

In the final mile of our next race, we'll assign four or five teammates to go to the front of the peloton and form a paceline. We'll want them to pick up the pace so that we get the train rolling faster and faster over the last kilometer. If they do this right, they will make the pace of the race so high that no other rider can attack. "Blistering" is how fast the pace should be. Meanwhile, George will be sitting in fifth position waiting for the perfect moment to unleash his sprint.

Each rider will be required to take just one short, very fast "pull" on the front. They won't need to rotate through this paceline because they're only going far enough to deliver George to the finish line.

With each rider taking a pull for about 200 meters, he can empty his fuel tank with the effort. They each should be going as fast as is smoothly possible so that George isn't wasting any energy. He'll need everything he can muster when it's time to sprint because even though the pace is fast now, it's going to get even faster when the sprinters start. When the lead rider can't pull anymore, his job is done and he simply pulls to the side and watches the pack go by.

So our sprinter, George, sits in the fifth position behind four red teammates, keeping his nose out of the wind until the last possible moment. If we've done it right, George will be the second rider in line when he unleashes his fierce sprint. It's a classic team maneuver. With incredible loyalty, everyone sacrifices his own chance of winning to help George win. All George needs to do during the final kilometer is keep his eyes open for anyone trying to sprint past him. When he crosses the line with his arms raised in victory, we all share the excitement. And then we will all go find him and ask for a share of the prize money.

Keep in mind, though, that the blue and green teams will be attempting to hatch similar plans, not to mention the orange, yellow, purple, and chartreuse teams. We have plenty of variations and plenty of tricks to employ during the final sprint. If we think we're the only ones who have a plan, we are complete idiots. Therefore, the lead-out is a frantic fight for position among all contenders in the race. It gets crazy when there are eight or nine teams trying to pull this off simultaneously on a roadway that's twenty-two feet wide.

The lead-out is the most basic tactic to use at the end of a race. It can be done with the assistance of any number of teammates. It can also be done without any teammates at all. A smart rider who has no teammates can play off the team tactics of other riders in the race by knowing what to look for and by taking the chance of predicting what other riders will do. If his prediction is right, he'll eat like a king. If not, well, that's bike racing!

PLAY TO YOUR STRENGTHS

Each team must determine which tactic works best for it based on the riders' abilities. Not every rider is strong. Not every rider is quick. Not every rider is smart.

O SOLO MIO

The sprint and the lead-out aren't the only ways to beat other riders. If you don't possess the ability to sprint and your team has no sprinter, then you'll need to employ some other tactics.

One way to win a bike race without a sprint is to launch a solo breakaway. This is a tactic that our nonsprinter, Larry, might want to try. First, he must take three factors into consideration. For starters, he must be able to create a gap between himself and the rest of the peloton. Second, he must time his attack when he thinks he can make it to the finish line successfully, that is, ahead of everyone else. (There's nothing worse than biting off more than you can chew and running out of energy before the finish line.) Third, Larry must have the ability to ride steadily at 90 percent or better for a long time.

I have to emphasize the different types of abilities that riders possess. Sprinters can accelerate very quickly. They are blessed with fast-twitch muscles that allow them to jump from cruising speed to top speed in a few pedal strokes. The downside is that what they get in speed, they give up in endurance.

The time trialists, named after the type of event in which they specialize (the time trial), can ride at a high speed for long periods of time, but it may take them some time to reach that high speed. Very rarely will you find a time trialist who can sprint, and vice versa.

Think of it in terms of fighter jets and long-range bombers. Fighter jets can take off on short runways. They can go supersonic, but their range is limited. Bombers may take longer to leave the ground and climb to cruising altitude, but they can stay in the air for hours.

Mountain goats are riders who can climb hills all day.

Riders who have no particular strengths are field fodder. They know how to race, but they have no ace card to play. They must rely on their smarts, experience, good looks, and luck.

The differences among these four types of riders are substantial.

When?

It is unlikely that the field would allow a single rider to simply ride away from it, so Larry will have to catch it by surprise. Imagine a group of 150 riders all looking in the same general direction, and Larry is supposed to find a way to surprise them. Believe it or not, it can be done. There are times when the field is susceptible to such an attack.

Many times during the course of a bike race, the field will go through extended periods of breakneck speeds. Sometimes there are sustained efforts at 90 percent or more that last for several minutes. But it really wears out everyone in the field to go that hard for an extended time.

Eventually the pace slows and the field relaxes. Collectively, the field will want a chance to recover; no one will want to crank it back up to 90 percent right away, and few will be physically able to. If Larry has the legs and lungs to do it, this is the best time to dig deep within and launch a solo attack. If the timing is right, it might stick.

We call this move a flyer. Larry is "taking a flyer" or "going on a flyer." It would be redundant to say that Larry "went on a solo flyer," since the word "flyer" refers to any solo attack, usually one of short duration.

A flyer may stretch into a solo breakaway or may become a full-blown breakaway as other riders bridge across to it. Or it may get caught soon after it forms.

Intimidating View

When Larry attacks, he will peek over his shoulder to see how the peloton responds. When he does, he's likely to see two different scenarios. In the first scenario, he'll see the field spread wide across the road and no one pedaling. This means they're not reacting to his attack. They're waiting to see what he's up to. In the second scenario, he'll see a single-file line of riders chasing after him at high speed. This is, perhaps, one of the most intimidating scenes in the sporting world. Larry will know what it's like to be an escaped prisoner. All that's missing is bloodhounds and prison guards with rifles.

NO NEED TO DECOY, ROY

Before I put the wraps on this topic, I must tell you that the flyer/solo breakaway is a tactic that teams sometimes use to wear down the opposition. The red team will send a rider, almost like a decoy, on a flyer, causing the blue and green teams to take up the chase. As soon as the first red rider is caught, the red team will send another rider on a flyer. Again, the other teams will organize a chase. When the second red rider is caught, guess what happens. Right! Red attacks again with a third rider. And again. And again. The objective is to wear down the blue and green teams so that eventually the red team can launch a serious attack by its strongest candidate. By then, it hopes, some of the starch will have been taken out of competitors' legs. (That's a phrase you may only hear in cycling. I have no idea where it came from.) With the competition weakened, Larry's attack may have a better chance of succeeding.

Be aware, though, that every team comes into the race with a strategy. We're not the only ones trying to outsmart our opponents.

UNATTACHED

If bike racing is a team sport, you may wonder how a lone rider stands a chance. (The U.S. Cycling Federation labels these riders as "unattached" because they aren't associated with a team.) A smart unattached rider will be able to identify opportunities and position himself to take advantage of certain situations. A smart rider who has no teammates might do well to form an alliance with other riders who have no teammates.

When two or more riders pool their efforts to form a team, we refer to it as a "combine" (pronounced like the farm implement: COM-bine). These combines are sometimes formed in the parking lot prior to the race. Sometimes they are formed at the starting line. Other times, they are formed a few days before a race when someone phones a friend who belongs to a different team. For example, "Hey, Todd, are any of your teammates going to the race in Traverse City next week? I'm going alone, and I'm looking for someone to work with."

If you find it interesting that Roadies form these ad hoc teams, you will be completely flabbergasted to know that they also form combines with total strangers while the race is under way! Sometimes riders from two rival teams form a combine. No, I am not kidding. It is testimony to the fact that cycling is indeed a team sport; riders will instantly band together if they can find any benefit in doing so. This alliance between rival teams extends far beyond a breakaway situation. They will actually devise team strategies with one another to further their own cause.

To form a combine, a rider must know instantly what's involved in doing so. It means that riders must quickly determine who will have what role. Riders have to know how to employ a variety of tactics. And finally, they must go into it with the assumption that they will split all prize winnings evenly when the race is done. And because we're talking about human beings here, I might suggest verbalizing that last point before the race gets too far along.

FINAL LAP

So far, I've told you about the breakaway, the mass sprint, the lead-out, the combine, the chase, and the solo attack. You now know that:

- Riders use the paceline as an efficient means of maintaining a high speed.
- A rider will try to improve his odds of winning by getting in a breakaway with people he has a chance of beating.
- Teams will try to get one of their riders into a breakaway and then try to block other teams from catching it.
- Teams will set up their fastest sprinter to finish a race, and by doing so they will sacrifice their own chances.
- Two or more riders from opposing teams will spontaneously form a combine.
- Some riders are better suited for a long, gutsy, solo effort.
- There are no restrictions on when these tactics can begin. When the starter's pistol is fired, let the games begin!

This chapter will take on new meaning as you read about the different race formats in upcoming chapters.

8. Crashes

As much as I'd like to ignore this topic, I can't. It's too important in the life of a Roadie. Ask any Roadie to tell you the story of his worst crash, and you will open up a large can of worms. Every Roadie has at least one long, drawn-out story to tell on the topic. Maybe more.

The aim of this chapter is to provide you with insight into all that's involved in crashing so that you will be better prepared to cope when the Crash Monster rears its ugly head. It may also help you to cope with the nervousness that often accompanies such a hairy sport.

CRASH HAPPENS

I've talked to a zillion nonracing cyclists over the years, and the one thing I've heard most often is that the threat of crashing is their number-one reason for choosing not to race. (The second-most-popular fear is of being dropped and humiliated.) A crash is an ever-present danger in bike racing and a possibility each rider faces every time the starter's pistol is fired. But it's no reason to miss out on the fun.

Many recreational (nonracing) cyclists do everything a racer does—train just as hard, watch their diet, tweak their bike, and so forth—but they do not make that short walk to the registration tent to sign up for a bike race. If they were to take the

time to learn how racing works from top to bottom, then the prospect of crashing would fade into the background.

It's a mistake to think that crashes are limited to Roadies and racing. Crashes are an inherent risk in cycling. Anytime you place a body on a two-wheeled device with a high center of gravity that requires a certain degree of balance, you can expect an occasional mistake. A cyclist who never enters a bike race for fear of crashing is kidding himself if he thinks he doesn't face the same risk in his everyday training. Crashes happen in every hallway of cycling.

The longer a Roadie is involved in the sport, the more crash stories he has. Good stories and bad. Funny and sad. Most crashes are as harmless as a bad hair day, but things can go from bad to horrible in a matter of seconds.

Perhaps there is an official document kept in a filing cabinet somewhere in the basement of the Office of Cycling Data that indicates the most common cause of bike race crashes. I could provide you with a list of common causes, but to identify one as the most common would only start an argument. Instead, let me divide crashes into categories:

- Corner crashes
- Straight-liners
- Other

I may not cover every angle of this topic, but we'll get a conversation started.

CORNER CRASHES

Corner crashes take place in and because of corners. I divide them into four subcategories:

- Conflicting lines
- Centrifugal force
- Loss of traction
- Clipped pedal

Conflicting Lines

A large pack of Roadies riding through a turn is an amazing sight. They move like a school of fish or a flock of birds as they negotiate a turn, wordlessly agreeing on which arc to follow. It is a beautiful thing—until one person follows a different arc, one that conflicts with the majority. Then they run into each other and fall down.

Centrifugal Force

Another way to lose control in the corner is to carry too much speed into it and allow centrifugal force to take over. This simply means that the riders' momentum takes them too wide through the exit apex. Unable to make the turn, they usually run into whatever may be waiting for them at the outside of the arc: a bale of hay, a lamppost, a tree, another rider, a spectator, a barricade, an ATM, the YMCA, and so on.

Loss of Traction

When a bike changes direction, it has a natural tendency to lean. The faster the bike travels, the more it will need to lean to negotiate a turn. The more a bike leans, the less traction its tires will have on the road. It is certainly possible to exceed the tires' ability to grip. When a rider attempts to turn too fast, the tires can slip out from under him even under the best conditions. If you add outside agents such as water, sand, or gravel to the mix, it's easy to lose contact. Believe me when I tell you that many different substances have caused crashes in bike races.

A Roadie's least favorite substance is the seemingly innocuous white paint that marks pedestrian crossings. In many cases, it's not paint but a thick rubbery substance that is melted onto the road surface. When it gets worn smooth by years of pedestrian and vehicular traffic, it can become a bike racer's nightmare, especially in the rain.

Another culprit is the manhole cover. These things always show up in the corners because that's where the public utilities are situated under the road. In recent years, the companies that manufacture manhole covers have added some texture to their covers, but I can assure you that millions of iron manhole covers remain in use that have been polished smooth by years and years of automobile traffic.

Clipped Pedal

When a bike leans to negotiate a turn, a pedal is the part of the bike closest to the ground when they are in the lowest point of their rotation. You can probably guess what's going to happen if a rider pedals through a corner at a high speed. If the bike is leaning too much, the pedal will come in contact with the ground. We call this "clipping a pedal."

If the pedal jams into the pavement hard enough, it will send the rear wheel into the air and launch the rider sideways. If one rider scrapes a pedal and gets thrown out of line, a chain reaction of crashing riders can result. The opportunity for this type of crash comes every time riders negotiate a turn at high speeds. Remember that in a race such as the criterium, riders are flying through 90-degree turns constantly at a high rate of speed. An experienced Roadie knows at precisely what speed he can pedal through a turn and at what speed he must coast. It is usually the inexperienced rider who subordinates the laws of physics to his desire to pedal through the turn.

An IRONIC TWIST

Corners are where we see a large percentage of crashes, particularly in the criterium event. Oddly, most riders seldom practice the art of cornering. Throughout the summer, they race 95 percent of their races on tight courses with sharp turns, yet they spend 0 percent of their training time working on corners. Why? Because they fear crashing. Isn't that ironic? They fear crashing, yet they don't bother to hone the skills needed to avoid it. Instead of finding a training route that has corners, they train on a straight country road.

It makes no sense whatsoever. But that's bike racing! And it's comforting to know that this trend appears in other sports, too. Recreational golfers spend all day on the driving range whacking long drives but neglect working on their short game (pitching, chipping, and putting), which is where their score lives and dies. That's golf.

STRAIGHT-LINE FEVER

Another major type of bike crash occurs when the field is riding in a straight line. For this reason, I cleverly call them straight-liners. The most common culprit here is the overlapped wheel. This happens when the front wheel of one rider comes alongside the rear wheel of another rider. Then the front rider drifts to the left or right and runs into the trailing rider's wheel, essentially sweeping the trailing rider's bike out from under him.

Another type of straight-liner results when handlebars become entangled. We usually see this at the novice level when riders are still getting used to the spatial relationships involved with bike racing. This kind of crash can be scary because it usually isn't instantaneous. Instead, both riders (and usually the riders around them) have a moment to realize the gravity of their situation. It's kind of like when the Road Runner has tricked Wile E. Coyote into driving over a cliff. Just before the coyote drops from sight, he holds up a small sign that reads, "Oh no!"

Remarkably, handlebars can sometimes come untangled, thus rendering this a nonevent. Novice riders should gracefully accept this as an opportunity to learn the lessons without the consequences of a crash.

O OTHER, WHERE ART THOU?

Crashes that fall under the heading of "Other" range from the dog-escapes-owner-and-runs-out-into-the-peloton crash to the popular someone-drops-their-water-bottle-and-chaos-ensues crash to my all-time favorite, I-pulled-my-foot-in-the-sprint crash.

The first two are self-explanatory. The last one requires a brief explanation. To "pull a foot" does not mean grabbing a foot and giving it a yank, though that might actually help some riders go faster. It means that a shoe unexpectedly and accidentally disengages from the pedal at an inopportune time. It usually happens when extra force is being applied to the pedals, as in a sprint—the least opportune time.

VOTED MOST LIKELY TO

Ask any Roadie to name the most common crash-related injury, and you may hear differing opinions. Most Roadies will agree that road rash and abrasions on the hips and calves are among the most common injuries. The bone broken most easily is the collarbone because it's one of the first things to hit the ground, and it only takes twelve pounds of pressure to snap it like a pretzel. A more common injury is gravel becoming embedded in the palm of the hand. This happens when Roadies start to

fall and instinctively reach out to catch themselves. This usually leads to more serious injuries such as a broken arm, elbow, or collarbone.

In the jumble of bikes and bodies of a crash, scrapes and abrasions can appear anywhere on the body. Ask any Roadie to tell you of the strange injuries sustained while racing. This might be a good subject to bring up at a party.

YOU'LL HEAR IT BEFORE YOU SEE IT

The noise that accompanies a crash is something you will come to recognize instantly. It's a high-pitched squeal, a combination of metal and rubber being scraped across pavement. It is a distinctive sound that temporarily trumps all else. In an instant, each Roadie will look for an escape route to avoid being caught in the crash or behind it. If you can't escape the crash, aim for something that can cushion your fall, such as a shrub, a lawn, a hay bale, or another body.

Where novice riders allow the specter of a crash to loom over them like threatening storm clouds, good riders deal with crashes by learning how to avoid them. They also learn how to minimize the damage when they do happen. Most importantly, they learn that no matter how much they try to avoid them, they can happen at any time, and that we're all at the mercy of the cycling gods.

Oddly, some riders get terribly upset when a crash affects their race, which is a lot like living in Alaska and getting upset when it snows. You can let it ruin your day, or you can learn to accept it as a fickle finger of fate.

GETTING BACK UP

Immediately upon crashing, riders begin assessing the damage. First, of course, they must check their bike to see that it's all in one piece. Eventually they assess their body for damage. Most Roadies will tell you that it has to be a severe injury to prevent them from continuing.

Don't be surprised if you see a rider pick himself up off the road with blood streaming down his leg from a severed artery, climb back on his bike, and ride as if he's outrunning a tornado. Adrenaline has a remarkable ability to numb pain or at least stave it off. Riders may not even realize they're hurt until after the race, when the adrenaline subsides. Until then, they seem to function as if nothing happened.

SLIP AND SLIDE

Most riders hate to race in the rain. It's dangerous. It's nerve-racking. A rain-soaked street can be as slippery as a skating rink. Oddly, crashes that occur on wet roads tend to be less harmful because bodies slide more easily across wet pavement. Road rash is therefore less severe on a rainy day.

CRASH-PRONE

I have a few random observations regarding crashes. I offer them to you as a means of starting conversations between you and your Roadie.

First, there is a huge difference between a crash in a Category I–II race and a crash in a Category IV race. Often a Category I–II crash involves two or three riders despite the fact that 120 riders are packed into the space of a school bus, but a similar crash in a Category IV race will take out several riders. Inexperienced riders are usually so tense and uptight that they overreact to any crash event. If one rider falls, five or six riders will run into him and also fall. Nearby, other riders panic and fall because of the noise from the first crash. Before you know it, there will be twenty riders on the ground.

Experienced riders know to relax and roll with it. They develop a sixth sense that allows them to anticipate and react to a crash as it's happening to avoid being involved. That's not to say that Category I–II riders aren't capable of putting on a demolition derby. They certainly are. But, with all else being equal, a Category IV crash will be more involved due to the inexperience of the riders.

Second, mountain bike riders tend to see Roadies as stuck-up, elitist, and snooty. Oh, sure, Roadies can be cold and unwelcoming to a new rider in contrast to mountain bike riders, who welcome new riders like pledges during rush week. I believe there is a simple and logical explanation for this. Roadies ride in such close proximity to one another that it's important for them to know whom they're riding with and whether or not another rider is a threat to personal safety. Until a new rider proves he's a safe rider, Roadies will give him a wide berth.

In the sport of mountain biking, riders seldom see each other once they're out on the trails, so who cares if some guy is careening into every other tree? As long as they make it out of the parking lot safely, there's nothing to worry about. They can be friends from the outset.

Third, several days after a crash, it's not uncommon for a Roadie to find an odd scar on a strange part of his body. As he replays the crash in his mind over and over again, he will be unable to figure out how it got there. For example, I know a rider who found a black mark behind his ear that we think came from someone's tire. There's no way for us to re-create the scene, so we can only guess.

Fourth, a Roadie who crashes will get sympathy from other Roadies for a day or two. Barring a hospitalization, we fully expect to see him at the next race. In reality, recovering from a crash, both physically and mentally, can take a long time. Racing takes nerve, and those nerves sometimes get shaken. In Roadieland, we'll give you two days.

And finally, crashing is expensive. In tennis, when things go wrong, you may break a string. When things go wrong in golf, you may lose a ball or wrap your club around a tree in frustration. In cycling, there are few inexpensive repairs. When a rider crashes, his reaction is to check his bike first and his body second. The body heals. The bike costs.

FINAL LAP

Any Roadie who refuses to work on the skills that will lessen the likelihood or the severity of a crash is participating in the sport less than fully prepared. And any cyclist who gets overly upset when the fickle hand of fate throws a curveball in the form of a crash is wasting energy. Just hope that the next crash isn't serious.

PART THREE
SUPPORTING ROLES

9. Race Day

In this chapter, I explain the routine that a Roadie goes through on the day of a race and how it affects the rest of his life as well as the lives of those around him. Even though a Roadie has signed up for a one-hour race, his entire day is devoted to it.

We'll follow our not-so-fictitious friend, George, through a normal routine.

A DAY IN THE LIFE

George's pre-race routine begins days in advance of the race with concerns about resting, stretching, and proper hydration and nutrition. If the race is an important season objective, the routine may start weeks in advance. It becomes more focused beginning with the meal on the evening before the race. If George has a date on the night before a race, it's probably going to be limited to sit-down activities such as dinner and a movie. Don't expect him to go out dancing and barhopping. Everything he does will be based on keeping his legs fresh and his energy level high. He will want to have his body ready to go when the starter's pistol is fired. If the race begins early in the morning, then most Roadies will spend the preceding evening preparing, planning, and packing.

BAGS ARE PACKED

Ask any Roadie how many times he has arrived at a race site missing a critical piece of gear. No matter how organized, methodical, or fastidious a rider may be, he will forget an important item sometime in his career. There's not a Roadie in America who hasn't forgotten something as important as his shoes or front wheel. There is so much junk a Roadie must remember to take with him to every single race that it's nearly impossible to get it right every single time, especially during the first few attempts.

Though I've never been a fan of checklists, I understand that some people thrive on them. Because George uses a written checklist, he will arrive at the race site with everything ready to race.

I COULD HAVE SWORN IT WAS JUST PAST THE AMOCO STATION

George needs to find the racecourse. This may seem like a simple thing, especially with the advent of online mapping programs and global positioning systems that can pinpoint the precise location of any address, waypoint, or longitudinal point in the world. However, bike races are never held at an address; they're held at a wide spot in the road. There may be a million businesses nearby whose address could be used as a guide, but instead, a primitive hand-drawn map or a set of cryptic written instructions will be included on the race flyer. George will use this to find the course.

As I've said, with all the stuff a Roadie must pack into the car for a day trip to a bike race, it's understandable that something may get left behind. Ask any Roadie, and he will tell you about the time he drove off and left his map on the kitchen counter. He was then forced to find the course using his bike racer instincts. It is not something a local resident can tell you.

You: Excuse me. Can you tell me how to get to the bike racecourse?
The Local: The what?

End of conversation.

Without a map, a Roadie will instinctively look for road closure signs, orange cones, detour signs, and anything else that may indicate a disrupted traffic pattern—hay bales, yellow plastic caution tape, barricades, other cars with bike racks, riders on bikes, and pop-up tents. It is possible to find a bike race without a map. George will do it this way until he writes the word "map" on his checklist.

DUDE, WHERE'S THE CAR? NO, SERIOUSLY. WHERE IS IT?

Though it may seem like a minor point, many Roadies put some thought into where they park the car in relation to the race site. The car will be their base of operations

for the entire day. It is where their equipment, food, water, and clothing are kept. Despite the importance they place in it, it will play no role in their overall success. It's purely a matter of convenience, thus no wasted energy.

It's a little bit like selecting a campsite. The challenge is to find the perfect balance among solitude, functionality, socialization, efficiency, and protection from the elements. During our family camping trips, for example, my dad had a knack for instinctively selecting a campsite located between a motorcycle gang and a church group, usually miles from a bathroom and the beach.

- *Secret Tip 1:* Do not park in an area that will result in a parking ticket. They issued parking tickets on the day the pope came to town, so they will definitely be writing tickets on bike race day. It's self-defeating to receive a $50 parking ticket on a day when you may win a grand total of $40.
- *Secret Tip 2:* Assess the security of the area before establishing your campsite. On a day when you may win $40, you do not want to lose a $5,000 bicycle to thieves.

- *Secret Tip 3:* If the race is held in a downtown area on a Sunday, as many criteriums are, I like to set up my race camp in a bank parking lot. Closed to business on Sundays, the covered drive-through teller lane makes the perfect camp. The overhang offers protection from the sun and rain. Also, there's an ATM nearby in case you receive your winnings in check form.

Roadies put great thought into things like this, but it's all for naught. In reality, they're usually running late and must park the car in the first available spot so that they can jump out and run like mad to the registration tent.

WHAT YOU CAN DO

If you are a spectator or a friend of a Roadie, you will be the keeper of the keys. At some point before the start of the race, the Roadie will thrust the car keys in your direction. Hold on to them. They will come in handy if you want to drive home. Also make a note of where the car is parked. You'd be surprised to know how easy it is to lose track of this small detail on race day.

PAY HERE

To participate in the race, George must sign up and pay an entry fee for the race he wishes to ride. It involves proving his membership by showing his USCF license, paying the fee, filling out the entry form, signing the liability waiver, receiving his race bib number, and picking up some safety pins.

Registration usually takes place under a tent located within sight of the start/finish area. That's the most convenient place for it. Every now and then, however, a promoter will get the crazy idea to place the registration tent in a quiet area far away from the action. This usually causes problems because riders hate to walk anywhere unnecessarily.

If George happens to be the only person in line at the registration table,

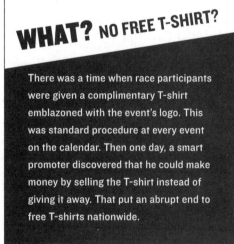

WHAT? NO FREE T-SHIRT?

There was a time when race participants were given a complimentary T-shirt emblazoned with the event's logo. This was standard procedure at every event on the calendar. Then one day, a smart promoter discovered that he could make money by selling the T-shirt instead of giving it away. That put an abrupt end to free T-shirts nationwide.

the entire process should take ninety seconds, provided he didn't leave his license at home. Unfortunately, it's not uncommon to see riders waiting in lines longer than those in the toy department at Macy's on the day after Thanksgiving. If George gets through the process quickly, he'll have more time to socialize with the other riders, inspect the course, get dressed, and go to the bathroom.

TAKE A LOOK AT TURN 4

One of the more time-consuming tasks that must be accomplished prior to a race is the course inspection. A few riders leave it out of the routine altogether, but most riders will want to be familiar with all three opponents: (1) riders, (2) elements, (3) terrain.

If it's a short course such as a criterium (see Chapter 12), the inspection can be done on foot in a matter of minutes. A simple walk around the course will be enough to show which corners are tricky, which lanes are bumpy, which areas will be affected by wind, which hills are challenging, and which areas will require more concentration.

If it's a long course, such as a road race (see Chapter 13), the inspection will require driving a car. Roadies will be looking for safety hazards, tactical elements, challenging features, and the final approach to the finish line. It's good to remove as many surprises as possible.

The degree to which a Roadie will inspect a course is related to the importance of the race and where it falls on his season objectives. If it's an important race, he will study the course like it's the state bar exam. On the other hand, if it's just a casual weekend race, he may skip the pre-race inspection with the idea of looking it over during the first few laps of the race.

PREPPING THE BIKE

George must ready the bike for competition before he puts on his racing uniform. If he has maintained his bike properly, this exercise will be simple:

> Step 1: Remove the bike from the car.
> Step 2: Ensure that the wheels are mounted and fastened properly.
> Step 3: Ensure proper air pressure in the tires. (A Roadie's tires
>   are capable of operating with air pressure hovering at
>   about 130 psi. Basically, he pumps them up until he thinks
>   they're about to explode, then he adds another 10 psi!)

Step 4: Wipe the bike down with a rag to make it look cleaner.

Step 5: Make sure everything works.

With the bike ready to go, the next step is to prepare the spare wheels. These wheels will be delivered to the support van or wheel pit sometime prior to the race. Because they will be kept with a thousand other spare wheels, they should have a simple means of identification on them, something that can be seen clearly from a distance in a panic situation. (I'll explain more about this later.)

TALKING 'BOUT THE WEATHER

Somewhere among the registration tent, the bathrooms, the warm-up, and the race, there will be a large amount of socializing among competitors. The topics will range from today's weather to new equipment. Early in the season, they'll talk about the past winter and how much training they did or didn't do.

TELLTALE SIGNS

The secret to detecting a sandbagger is to look for the telltale signs of training. First, if a rider has defined tan lines on his face, neck, and legs, there is a pretty good chance he has been spending time on the bike. Second, if the Roadie is thin and the skin on his face is taut, then he's been training. It's hard to hide fitness.

SANDBAGGER'S BALL

Ask any Roadie about his training, and he will lie to you. It goes something like this:

Rider 1: So, how's it goin'?
Rider 2: Not so good. I haven't been riding much. I was off the bike for a couple of weeks. I haven't been sleeping well. I haven't been eating right lately. I had a stomach virus. I've been working extra hours at the bike shop.

None of this is true. Rider 2 is sandbagging. It is a rare bird that will come to a race and proclaim, "I've been training like a madman! I am *so* ready for this race! I've never felt this good!"

If they are indeed ready, they don't want you to know.

Third, a less obvious sign of a true Roadie is the area just above the knee where the quadriceps muscle ends. When a Roadie has been riding a lot, this skin tends to sag slightly when he is standing up straight. This skin actually gets stretched out by repetitive pedaling. If this flap is easy to detect, then you can be assured that the owner has been riding a lot.

WINDOW DRESSING

George should now be getting dressed. Though this may seem like a simple task, Roadies can goof it up quite easily. First of all, since the race is held on public roads, there is no locker room for riders to use.

Most Roadies get dressed in the relative privacy of their car. Unfortunately, aside from a delivery van, there is no vehicle on the market that comfortably accommo-

dates wardrobe changes, so the cloth-ing never really gets onto the body in the correct way. As a result, the cyclist will spend ten minutes readjusting his shorts until everything is where it needs to be. Don't make fun of him as he does this. He may fidget more than a five-year-old boy in church on a hot day; just accept it as part of the game and move on. Ask any Roadie; there is noth-ing worse than uncomfortable shorts.

A PINNING CEREMONY WITHOUT ALL THE SINGING

Before George puts on his jersey, he must pin the race number to it. This is obvi-ously done for identification purposes. Consequently, Roadies collect hundreds of paper numbers over the course of their career.

There are two schools of thought about pinning the number onto the jersey. Roadies who subscribe to the first school take care of this task before they put on their jersey. These riders are self-sufficient, organized, and capable. They require no assistance from anyone. They carefully position the number and pin it to the jersey while it's lying on their lap. Some treat this as a Zen-like ritual that helps them get their mind into the race mode. Many riders use this quiet time before the race as a communal vibe, a tribal meeting time when they can discuss the approaching race much like at the quilting bees that American settlers participated in while discussing the upcoming harvest.

The other school of thought is to have someone else pin the number on the Roadie while the pre-race announcements are being presented. Forget about relaxing, focusing, and concentrating; this is a frantic last-minute afterthought. Many riders use this as a means of involving their friends and family, which I think is great, but I need to point out some dangerous risks.

The first risk is simple. Though technically it is called a safety pin, whoever is doing the pinning may accidentally poke the rider with the sharp end of the pin. Riders are funny about this. They are about to spend at least an hour on the bike experiencing the depths of pain and agony, yet they howl like a coyote if poked with a pin. The second risk is also simple. By inadvertently pinning the number on upside down, you will cause your rider to be harangued by the rest of the peloton. Also be aware that the number should never be pinned to the front of the jersey. It should always appear on the back panel of the jersey oriented in a way to make it visible to the officials.

OLD NUMBERS ADD UP

Many riders save every bib number they've ever worn and make notes on the back about each race. For example: "Ann Arbor Criterium, June 16, 1996. 21st place. Bad starting position. Felt awful. Chased a few breakaways. Got stuck behind a crash with ten laps to go. Felt better toward the end. Tried to give Mark a lead-out, but got pinched in the final turn. Finished one place out of the money."

THE WARM-UP

In the last half hour before race time, George should be warming up—riding around somewhere near the course or on the course if permissible. He needs to use this time to get his heart rate up and the muscles ready for the pain that is to come. This means different things to different people. Some riders require a lot of time to warm up; two hours is not uncommon. Others can do it in ten minutes. Some riders like to do several short sprints; others prefer to do one long, hard effort. To each his own. Each rider has to determine what's best for him. Of all the things we'll concern ourselves with today, this is the most important.

So now, for better or worse, George has registered himself for the race. He has received his number and pinned it to his jersey. He's gotten dressed. He's inspected the course. He's prepared the bike. He's warmed up. He's done all the last-minute fidgets. Now we're waiting to report to the starting line.

"RIDERS TO THE LINE"

This is the call that sends shivers down the spines of Roadies everywhere. The announcement is made calling all riders (in the upcoming race) to the starting line. Every rider should go there directly. The sooner you report to the start line, the better your starting position will be. It is first come, first served. There will be a short period spent listening to the USCF officials go through their pre-race declarations before the race starts.

In theory, riders should use those last few idle minutes to stretch the muscles, settle the nerves, drink some water, and get focused on the task at hand. In reality, all kinds of things take place in the final moments before the gun is fired, things that should have been taken care of much earlier in the day. At least one rider will be scrambling to pin his bib number on. Someone else will be screaming at his girlfriend to "get a fresh water bottle out of the car." Someone else will decide that

HOW **NOT TO**

At the 1999 U.S. National Championships in Cincinnati, Ohio, I saw three racers dash into the portable bathrooms just before the start of their race. These three riders each gave in to pre-race nerves and decided to use the bathrooms while their fellow racers were at the starting line receiving the pre-race ground rules.

While the three riders were occupied, their race was given the green light. The starter's pistol was fired, and the national championship race began. I watched as they each stepped out of the outhouse simultaneously and gaped in horror as their compatriots sprinted away from the starting line. They frantically clambered over the fencing that lined the course, jumped on their bikes, and chased in vain to catch up, already about thirty seconds behind. After four minutes of hell-bent but fruitless chasing, they found themselves so far out of contention that the race officials had no choice but to pull them from the race after only three or four laps.

In that one instant, they blew the previous eight weeks that they had spent ramping up for the national championships. Their hopes were dashed, and their season-long goal was for nothing.

now is the best time to put more air in the tires, and someone else will be frantically looking for a 5-mm Allen wrench to lower his saddle by a millionth of an inch (as if it would make any difference at this point). None of these things should delay the start, but it's perfectly normal if they do. Such is the flexibility of cycling. If a rider is running a little behind, it's not uncommon to hold the race until he's ready.

This would never happen in the NFL. When the television network says it's time for the game to start, the game starts. For example, a kickoff return specialist would never be allowed to take a minute just before the kickoff to hand his car keys to his wife in the crowd. But in cycling, it happens all the time.

Pre-race fidgets and last-minute scrambles are par for the course and are by no means limited to rookie racers. Nor are they the worst thing that can happen. There is a good probability that a rider will completely miss the start of a race at some point during his racing career.

So when the call to the line is made, George should have all of those last-minute things taken care of and be ready to race. There should be no last-minute scrambling of any sort. Of course I'm dreaming, but let's move on.

THE TRAIN LEAVES AT HIGH NOON

Just like an Amtrak train, a bike race cannot start prior to the time that is printed in the race flyer. Everything a Roadie does on race day will be centered on that golden time.

Let's be clear on one thing: This is a bike race, not a session of Parliament. Therefore, we allow some flexibility in the schedule. Although the race schedule states a definite start time, it's not uncommon for the riders to be called to the starting line several minutes early and be forced to stand there while they wait for the proper start time to come.

BANG!

Eventually—possibly on time, possibly not—the starter's pistol is fired and the race is under way. From this point on, George is racing. Everything leading up to this moment is just a prelude to the real thing. For many Roadies, this prelude (as well as what happens after the race) is as much a part of the allure as the race itself. Just like California surfers who hang out on the beach, wax their surfboards, and talk about big waves, Roadies appreciate the whole, not just the parts. This is part of what John Howard means in the quotation that appears in the preface. The seasonal

LATE; **NEVER** EARLY

I have seen only one race start before its appointed time. It was a small event in upstate New York in which officials were distracted by a number of Murphy's Law violations that had occurred throughout the day. By late afternoon, they were ripe for a mental breakdown.

Anxious to get the day over with, they inadvertently started the race ten minutes early. Some riders were still getting ready when the starter's pistol was fired. Such a donnybrook ensued between the race officials and the five or six racers who missed the start of the race that I'm sure it'll never happen again. Or at least I hope it doesn't happen again. Or if it does happen again, I hope I'm not there.

friendships and lasting unions, the accoutrements, the jargon, and so on all add up to create a lifestyle, a scene, and a happening. This isn't just a trip to the corner store. This is a major production, and it's not simply about the race itself.

FINAL LAP

I assure you that everything described in this chapter takes place at every race across America, with slight variations. Sometimes this egocentric routine causes Roadies to forget all about their supporters/friends/relatives/coworkers, thus leaving them out in the cold. If this is you, please don't take it personally.

I have omitted some of the rituals and superstitions that a Roadie may observe before he leaves the house. I've also avoided writing about his frame of mind as he goes through this pre-race routine. It's yet another good question to ask a Roadie.

I'll cover the post-race routine later in the book.

10. The System

Before we consider the different types of bike races, we need to look at the overall governance of road cycling. Under whose authority does it operate? What is its governing body? What holds it all together? And how does the framework affect riders? This is a complex subject that will require me to bounce around a lot as I explain it.

THE FEDS

The United States Cycling Federation (henceforth referred to as the USCF or the Federation) writes the rules that govern the amateur side of the sport. Covering the road cycling section under the umbrella of USA Cycling, it doles out race permits, sets rules and guidelines, and tells us how races should be run. It was known as the Amateur Bicycle League of America for years before becoming the USCF in 1976. These are the folks who grant racing licenses to bike racers in the United States.

If there is an amateur bike race held on a road in the United States, it will be overseen by the USCF. Professional road cycling events are governed by the U.S. Pro Cycling Federation (USPRO). Mountain bike races are governed by the National Off-Road Bicycle Association (NORBA). BMX racing falls under the BMX Association. All of these are covered by USA Cycling, located in Colorado Springs.

As cycling's governing body, the USCF is our link to the U.S. Olympic Committee. National teams, national championships, Olympic team qualification, and rider development programs are held under USCF auspices. On the national scale, the USCF assigns regional coordinators to oversee activities in five regions across the United States. This covers things like regional scheduling, rider categorization upgrades, coaching and training clinics, and disciplinary action against riders and clubs who break the rules.

On the local scale, the Federation issues permits to bike races and also trains, certifies, and assigns race officials to all bike races in the United States that hold a USCF permit. These officials are local people who either love bike racing, love spending their weekends at bike races, love the task of officiating, or are related to a bike racer and have found no better way to spend their weekends. They come from all walks of life and bring their own expertise to each race. As much as Roadies love to race, officials love to officiate. Race officials will be on hand to make sure that events are run in accordance with USCF rules and that riders adhere to them. Rules work for the good of all, and officials work for peanuts. Actually, they receive a stipend that almost covers the cost of aspirin. In other words, nobody is getting rich at officiating.

There are a million rules covering all aspects of racing. It's the responsibility of each and every Roadie to be familiar with the USCF rulebook and to abide by the rules. It is the responsibility of the officials to know and enforce the rules.

A typical officiating crew consists of three or four officials, including a chief referee who oversees the race, ends all disputes, enforces rules, and is generally the rock of levelheadedness and sound judgment. Under the watchful eye of the chief ref is the chief judge, who is in charge of producing accurate results for every race. The chief judge oversees the activities of the judges. The judges and referees watch the race closely to ensure that nobody cheats. They settle disputes and oversee the safe running of each race. Upon

DISCLAIMER

Actually, a couple of bodies govern cycling in the United States. The USCF was the only game in town until the mid-1990s, when a few regions decided to break free and form their own governing body. As of this writing, the USCF is still the top dog by a long shot, and the other groups are still regional in scope. Many riders who live in those regions hold licenses from both the USCF and the local governing organization and can compete in the events of both organizations. It's kind of like when your dad joined the Elks Club and the Rotary. He could go to both holiday parties as long as they weren't held on the same night.

I recognize the fact that there are other organizations. In this book, for the sake of simplicity, however, I'm going to use the USCF as the model.

completion of the race, they determine the correct finishing order of as many riders as necessary to cover the prize list. A larger event will have a larger officiating crew assigned to it. Small events may have only two or three officials.

I SECOND THAT PROMOTION

The next thing you need to know is how races are organized. If you're thinking that the USCF organizes and promotes every bike race in the country, you're way off the mark. The only races the USCF actually has a hand in organizing are the national championships. All other races in the country are organized by independent race promoters who go out into their community to find sponsors who will give them money so they can stage the events and give Roadies a place to race. Without these freelance organizers, our sport would not exist. Race promoters follow USCF guidelines but otherwise seldom interact with the Federation.

Self-Starters Wanted

There is no certification needed to become a race promoter, only desire, interest, and boundless energy. Organizational skills certainly help. Race promoters can be anyone in your community. For example:

- A local newspaper publisher: Bruce Mitchell of Athens, Ohio
- A local bike shop owner: Jeff Noftz of Clarkston, Michigan

- A municipal bicycle projects coordinator: Jamie Carmosino of Dayton, Ohio
- A career consultant: Paul Alman of Chelsea, Michigan
- A racer's brother: Rich Hincapie of Greenville, South Carolina
- A former bike racer: Jay Baumeister of Columbus, Ohio

Anyone who feels inspired to take on the role of race promoter is encouraged to do so. Also, each USCF-licensed club is required to promote a bike race. This means that a Roadie may be thrust into the position of race organizer or volunteer. If this happens, I should warn you that he may recruit family and friends to help out at these events. The only thing to keep in mind is that it tends to be thankless work. It also involves reinventing each event from the ground up.

That's bike racing!

Monumental Task

First, remember that there are no stadiums designed and built for road cycling, so the first thing that must be done is to find a location to hold the race. Acquiring permission to use the roads should be the first step in the process because without roads, we have no race.

Every Roadie in America knows a road that would make the perfect racecourse. While riding the many miles it takes to train for competition, they discover the perfect loop for a race. In most cases, however, that's as far as it gets. Few racers actually pursue the dream of holding a race on their perfect loop because they understand what is required to be a race promoter. Therefore, it is the race promoter who must chase down the required permission. With tentative approval to use the roads, a plan can be laid out that includes the proposed budget, goals and objectives, sponsorship acquisition, and possible dates.

QUICK STORY

Once upon a time, a race promoter sought permission to use some downtown streets for a bike race in Grand Rapids, Michigan. City officials demanded that the promoter provide an eight-foot Plexiglas barrier on both sides of the street around the kilometer-long course to protect spectators from harm. The barrier would have cost more than $50,000. The budget for the race was $8,000. The end.

Our first step will be to establish a budget to work from. In doing so, we will factor in the following items:

- Signage
- Promotion, including advertising
- Printing fees
- Announcer
- Sound system
- Finish-line results
- Police services
- Crowd-control fencing
- Tent rentals
- Registration
- Officials
- Food vendors
- Lunches for the volunteers
- T-shirts for the volunteers
- Portable toilets/waste management
- Duct tape
- Other things too mundane to list

A large portion of the budget will be dedicated to the purse. We refer to it as the prize list: money awarded to the top finishers. This single factor will determine the level of racing we can expect. If we offer a prize list of $500, we may attract riders from as far away as the neighboring county. On the other hand, if we offer a prize list of $10,000, we will attract racers from every state this side of the Mississippi/Rockies/Mason-Dixon Line.

The next step is to contact the USCF in order to secure a date on the calendar. The Federation makes every attempt to prevent conflicting race dates. It does the sport little good to have events bumping heads with each other.

Money Makes the Bikes Go 'Round

So far, we have a course and a date. The next thing we need is money. We are about to enter one of the most terrifying, exhilarating, defeating, soul-baring experiences in life. We're going to search for sponsors who will pick up the tab for our dream.

This is torture for some, fun for others. Either way, it is a huge task that involves convincing, selling, coaxing, massaging, nurturing, cultivating, communicating, promising, cajoling, begging, and groveling. We're asking companies that are in business to make money to give us money. To get them to do that, we have to prove that we have a product worth investing in. In return, we will give them exposure by painting their name on our bike race and leaving an indelible impression on those who attend our event. That's the plan, anyway.

Once we have cash in hand, we can begin to assemble all of the parts. Ironically, it's a lot like building a bicycle. Without all the parts, we can't ride.

CALLING ALL ROADIES

We need to notify all Roadies of our upcoming event. To do this, we will advertise our race in bike racing magazines and Web sites. With the help of a mailing list from the Federation, we can target licensed riders in the region by mailing race flyers to them.

Riders want to know something about the event as they plan their summer race schedule, for example, what the terrain is like, how much prize money is being awarded, which rider categories are featured, and whom to contact. All this information can be included in the race flyer or advertisement.

When offered the chance, most riders prefer to register in advance via an online registration form.

A FULL SLATE OF EVENTS

On the day of the race, there will be six or seven separate races on the schedule, with the first one beginning at 8:00 a.m. and the last one beginning at 4:00 p.m. Why? I can give you two solid reasons. First, the promoter may wish to include events for small children, celebrities, hand-cyclists, in-line skaters, and so on. Second, and most importantly, the promoter will attempt to provide races for every category and age group covered by the USCF.

Categorically Confusing

The Federation recognizes that all bike racers are not created equal and categorizes them according to ability, age, and gender. This creates a rather bizarre organizational chart and pecking order for which there is no easy explanation.

If you were to apply for a USCF amateur racing license today, you would be placed in Category V; that's our entry level. It's the lowest rung on the ladder. The top rung of that ladder is Category I, the cream of the crop in amateur racing. Be-

HOW TO SAY IT

Few riders use the word "category" when referring to ability level. It takes too much energy to move the tongue and lips and teeth. To a Roadie, that's energy better spent on the bike. Instead, we simply abbreviate it by saying "Cat. I" or "Cat. V." For example, "He's a Cat. IV rider." Or perhaps, "I'm racing Cat. IIIs today."

Notice the truncated semantics. The Roadie actually means, "I'm racing with the Category III racers today." However, we can save time and energy by omitting some words. Oh, how fresh and alive we'll feel later in the day if we keep trimming the language down to the most essential syllables! There is no need to pronounce all five whole tiresome syllables: cat-e-go-ry-three. Gosh! What a waste of energy!

yond the Category I level, a rider can get a professional racing license—or quit the sport and make his family happy by finding a real job. The climb up the ladder from Category V to Category I is a long road for some, shorter for others. Lance Armstrong, for example, flew through the lower categories with ease and went straight to the top rung. Others are not as fortunate.

So, What's the Difference?

The differences between the categories are significant. A Cat. V rider presumably lacks the speed, form, technique, intricacy, intensity, and sophistication to keep pace with the Cat. IIIs. For the same reason, a Cat. III rider would have a difficult time keeping pace with a group of Cat. Is. As such, Roadies wear their category ranking like a brand burned into their flesh. Varying degrees of status and honor are assigned to riders as they progress up through the rank structure. As the top dogs, Cat. I riders carry the most esteem. Cat. Vs take some heat for being novices.

In some ways, the relationship between a Cat. I rider and a Cat. V rider is similar to that between a senior and a freshman. The main difference, of course, is that seniors graduate and move on, but a Cat. I rider can just stay there and beat you again and again and again.

To make matters worse, a promoter may not have adequate time to provide a separate race for every category, so he may be forced to combine categories. The Federation allows this as long as it's done in sequence. For example, you may see

one race held for Cat. I–III and another race for Cat. IV–V. You may see a race for Cat. I–II and another race for Cat. III–V. However, you'll never see a race for Cat. I, III, and V and another race for Cat. II and IV, though it might be fun to watch!

ROCK OF AGES

The USCF also divides riders into age groups to keep things fair for the older riders and the younger riders. Age groups over thirty are called masters. Riders under eighteen are called juniors.

You may find it odd, though, that the USCF also gives masters, women, and juniors the option to race with their category in senior races. For example, rules allow a fourteen-year-old Cat. II racer to race in the junior race *and* in the senior Cat. II race by his choice. Similarly, a fifty-eight-year-old Cat. II racer can race with his category in a masters race and a senior Cat. II race by his choice. A woman Cat. II racer may, at the discretion of the chief referee, be permitted to race in a women's race and a senior Cat. II men's race on the same day.

As a result, it's entirely possible to have a bike race made up of men and women ranging in age from twelve to ninety-three. And because we frequently combine the amateur and professional riders, we can add pro racers to the mix. This happens often, and as crazy as it may sound, it works fine because bike races have a natural selection process of their own. Weaker riders are separated from the herd by their lack of speed and ability. In the mainstream sports, the weakest player in the game can have a profound effect on the outcome of a game. In cycling, the weak get dropped.

Would the National Hockey League ever try something like this? Not likely, but I'd pay good money to see it.

The Woman Conundrum

Women racers are also categorized by skill level and age. However, there is no professional level for them to reach due to the low number of women racers in North America. For that same reason, there is also no Category V. In many parts of the country, there are so few women racers that they often get lumped together into one women's field containing all four categories. Consider that point for a moment.

Imagine trying to compete against Mia Hamm in your first soccer tournament! Imagine entering your first tennis tournament and drawing Maria Sharapova in the first round. It's entirely possible for a woman bike racer to get crushed by the top female riders in the country during her first race. There aren't many negative things in this sport, but that qualifies as one of them. I can only hope that novice women crushed by elite racers don't sell their bikes and become soccer players. They may want to become mountain bikers. In a mountain bike race, everyone gets dropped except the winner.

Junior Mince

If we were to let all juniors race together, we would have some angry parents on our hands. Most fourteen-year-old kids don't stand a chance against seventeen-year-olds. Due to the wide disparity in development and ability, the USCF breaks the junior fields into two-year increments to help keep racing competitive. Age groups become ten- to eleven-year-olds, twelve- to thirteen-year-olds, fourteen- to fifteen-year-olds, and sixteen- to seventeen-year-olds. This is more equitable and a lot safer for the competitors. Unfortunately, due to the low number of participants, the junior racers usually get lumped together into one race (much like the women), leaving the twelve-year-olds to fend for themselves against the seventeen-year-olds. That's bike racing! Unfortunately.

Two for One

In an attempt to economize on time, race promoters often schedule the juniors to race concurrently with another group, such as the masters. For this reason, we often see two fields combined. Federation rules allow this, and it can be done in two different ways. The first method is to combine two age groups into a single race. The second method is to run two completely separate races on the course at the same time.

This confusing practice is not something we're accustomed to seeing in the world of sport. It works in bike racing, but it wouldn't work anywhere else. For example, at a baseball game, can you imagine hearing the public announcer say, "Good afternoon, ladies and gentlemen! It's my pleasure to welcome you here today for a baseball game between the Little League Widgets and the Senior Citizen Gray Ghosts. Also on the field today, we have the Sisters of Mercy playing against Brownie Troop 105! Batters up!"

It is up to the promoters to establish the race schedule. They must take into consideration all of the USCF categories when doing so, and use all of the aforementioned devices to make it happen. As such, the USCF gives the promoter some flexibility in operating the event.

PLANNING STAGES

When reading a race flyer, a Roadie will decide whether or not he wants to attend the event based on the following considerations:

- Is it close to home, or will it require overnight housing?
- How big is the prize list? Will I break even?
- Does the type of racing suit my type of riding?
- Is it a difficult course? Is it a dangerous course? Will I survive?
- Does the event have a good reputation? Is it well managed?
- Does it carry any prestige? Will winning it make me famous among my peers?

A rider considers other aspects of the event, too. Does it attract a decent-sized crowd? Does he know any other riders who will be attending? What will the weather be like? Does he have a chance of winning money? Or is he destined to get dropped altogether? Obviously our flyer can't answer all those questions.

CONTRACTING OUT THE TOUGH JOBS

By now, you can see that a promoter's job is extensive. There is a mountain of work involved in pulling together all of the items mentioned in this chapter. Depending on the size of the event, the promoter will either tackle the important technical elements of a cycling event on his own, or he'll farm them out to specialty companies that concentrate on specific event management tasks: photofinish camera/results, sound system, and announcing, to name a few.

The most important of the technical elements is results. It is imperative that every rider's finishing position within the prize list be accurately recorded. Though obtaining correct results is the duty of the officials, it behooves the race promoter to augment their efforts with technology, for he will be doling out the prize money to the top ten or twenty places when the race is over. Inaccurate results will cause guaranteed arguments.

PHOTOFINISH

There are four different techniques for capturing the finish of a bike race: human visual, video, digital capture, and computer-chip timing.

The most basic technique is human visual: Watch the finish of the race and write down the order of the finishers. This method was employed before the advent

NUMBER 1 ON YOUR PROGRAM

What number did Babe Ruth wear on his uniform throughout his career? What number did Brett Favre wear? What number did Hector Berlioz wear? Well, if you're expecting to recognize a Roadie by the number he wears, you're in for a letdown.

At every bike race, each rider has a number pinned to his jersey, usually on the back. Unfortunately for spectators, a Roadie never has the same number twice.

Little or no consideration is given to spectators' needs in this regard. The only real purpose the bib number serves is for identification of riders during the race by the officials. Officials need to see the number as they score the race, especially the finish. These officials are positioned on one side of the road at the finish line, which explains why the number appears only on one side of the rider's body.

So if John Elway ever decides to become a bike racer, it's doubtful that he'll wear his familiar number 7. He'll be assigned a random number every weekend, just like the rest of us.

---

of video cameras. Race officials would enlist volunteers to stand at the finish line and help them pick the order. For example, you might be asked to pick sixth and seventh place. That's easy if they're coming across in small groups, but not if they're finishing en masse. Imagine picking twentieth place! Or twenty-fifth! This method, although not foolproof, can be effective if the volunteers are honest and adept at watching a bike race.

Video is the cheapest and most readily available, but it's not entirely accurate due to the fact that video captures at a rate of thirty frames per second. You may be surprised to know that a lot can happen in a thirtieth of a second. I've seen some knock-down, drag-out fights occur among those reviewing the footage following close finishes. Still, this technique is used at a majority of races in the United States.

Digital-capture technology is limited to big-budget events. It consists of a high-speed camera sending images directly to a computer. It requires a trained staff to operate it, but it is instantaneous and accurate, making it today's system of choice.

Computer-chip timing is the newest technology to find its way into cycling. It involves attaching a transponder device to the bike, usually on the fork skewer or rider's ankle. A receiving device at the finish line records each transponder as it crosses the magnetic field.

This system works best in stage races based on accumulated time, such as the Tour de France, to keep track of the timing of all riders, but it falls far short in its

IT'S OFFICIAL, and That's FINAL

As the final sprint is taking place, the announcer will be disclosing the names of the winner, second-place finisher, and so on. He calls it as he sees it, but since he's a human being, he's prone to error.

In the moments following the end of the race, the announcer will probably repeat this information as he provides a recap to the audience. If he's wrong, he'll likely continue to be wrong until the officials provide him with correct information. Whatever the announcer says at this time is considered the "unofficial results" because the announcer is not an official but a chatty spectator with a PA system. (My apologies to race announcers everywhere.)

The officials produce their version—the official results—which are then announced over the PA system and posted in a central viewing area. This begins a fifteen-minute period during which riders have an opportunity to declare any protests and debate any discrepancies. If, based on a rider's protest, the chief judge changes the results, there is an additional fifteen-minute protest period. Barring further debate, the fifteen minutes elapse, and official results become final results.

ability to pick the order of a close finish. There are too many variables in the system to allow for accurate capture of the finishing order. For example, the USCF rule states that the finish of a race is determined by the leading edge of a rider's front wheel. But since there's no way to attach the chip to the leading edge, the results this system produces can never be truly accurate. For the record, I do not want to be around when an important race with a big prize purse comes down to millimeters if computer chips are used.

The key to accurate results, however, rests not with the technology but with the officials' ability to make sense of the information. It helps to have proper placement of the camera and proper placement of the riders' numbers on their bodies. Technology is useless if the camera cannot see what it needs to see. The camera must be mounted at the proper angle to be able to see (1) the finish line, (2) the front edge of front tires as they cross the line, (3) the bib numbers pinned to the riders' backs.

POSTING THE RESULTS

Using the method they are given, the officials determine the exact order of finish, and the list of names is posted in a central location for everyone to see. When the results are declared official and final, the promoter can distribute the prize list. We call this phase of the process "payout." Riders gather around like birds in a Hitchcock film as they receive their prize money.

Remember that many of the races are held on a Sunday, and that riders have to pay for meals, gas, and lodging. They won't find a bank that will cash a check on a Sunday. They'll need cash to pay for their trip home. They prefer to receive their prize money in cold, hard cash. Cash. Cash. Cash! But at 99 percent of races, they receive checks.

ON THE PODIUM

At the bigger events, the awards ceremony takes place immediately following the race while the crowd is still buzzing with excitement. The longer it takes to get the winner onto the podium, the fewer spectators will wait around. To help facilitate this, the officials will quickly verify the top three places before they complete the entire list. The top three finishers will be ushered onto the podium, handed flowers and a trophy, and asked a few questions by the announcer. While the ceremony is going on, the officials dedicate themselves to the task of completing the results. For them, there is no time to savor the pageantry. Their job isn't done until all results are posted.

FINAL LAP

At the end of the day, as Roadies are packing their gear and heading for home, the promoter has a chance to reflect on the day's events, replaying in his mind the things that went wrong and forgetting all that went right. He will likely vow never to attempt such a feat again. A few weeks later, though, he'll mail a crate full of thank-you notes and start making phone calls rounding up support for next year's event.

Roadies, on the other hand, will remain oblivious to all that took place behind the scenes to make the event happen. They tend to get wrapped up in their own routine.

That's bike racing!

11. Our Sponsors

Here's a story from the 1993 Fresca International Cycling Classic—Superweek—that formidable seventeen-day bike race in Wisconsin that I mentioned in Chapter 3.

As the television producer for the 1993 Superweek event, I created a sixty-minute recap of all seventeen days of racing. Among my varied responsibilities, I had to create the opening credits for the program with the accompanying voice-over that contains comments like, "The 1993 Superweek! Brought to you by . . . Fresca, the tasteful alternative . . . Saturn, a different kind of company, a different kind of car . . . Miller Lite, it's the right beer now . . . American Airlines, something special in the air . . ." and so on.

You missed it, didn't you? Don't worry. It was a glaring error that a lot of people missed because it passed by so quickly. I'll bet that if you go back and read it again, you'll miss it again. It's pretty subtle to us, but it's certainly not a mistake that would be taken lightly at Miller Lite headquarters. Ah, but they missed it, too.

You see, in 1993, Miller Lite wasn't "the right beer now"; it was "everything you've always wanted in a beer, and less." I wasn't aware of that because I'm not a beer drinker, and, ironically, I don't watch much TV. It sounded right to me when I produced the television program, so that was how I wrote it, that was how I voiced it, and that was how it aired. Forget the fact that Miller Lite probably spent thousands of dollars on focus groups to develop its slogan; I moved forward with whatever sounded good to me at the time. So much for focus groups!

The 1993 Fresca International Cycling Classic aired on local affiliates in Milwaukee and throughout Wisconsin with my mistake appearing in the first minute of the program. To make matters worse, Milwaukee is a beer town. Pabst, Schlitz, Miller, Leinenkugel, and Anheuser-Busch all have breweries in Milwaukee. The Major League Baseball team is called the Brewers. Laverne and Shirley worked at the fictitious Schotz brewery in Milwaukee. The fine folks of "Mill-town" really know and love their beer.

Obviously, to make that kind of mistake in a television program is a major thing. Heads roll for mistakes like this. Careers end for mistakes like this. But nobody ever noticed the mistake. The program aired with nary a complaint from anyone.

I'm not sure what that says about the Superweek program or cycling in general. It is, however, a fitting story to begin this chapter on sponsorship. The whole relationship between Roadies and their sponsors is rather odd and not always tidy. By the end of this chapter, you'll understand what I mean.

YOU SCRATCH MY BACK, I'LL SCRATCH YOURS

I'll start at the beginning by explaining why the amateur side of the sport of cycling includes the prominent display of sponsorship logos, business names, and product names while other sports, such as baseball, soccer, and running, do not. The reason is this: Cycling is expensive. I already explained how expensive it is in earlier chapters, so I'm not going to rehash that topic. But I will remind you that if you want to race competitively, you will need to take out a second mortgage on your home. Finding a sponsor who is willing to contribute money to defray some of the costs makes a Roadie's life a lot more affordable.

Instead of money, a sponsor may supply bicycle equipment or clothing, or may pay for travel expenses and entry fees. Some sponsors supply teams with product or in-kind services. It all depends on what kind of deal can be struck between the team and the sponsor.

Ideally, the relationship between team and sponsor should benefit both parties. The team receives the financial support it needs to compete, while the sponsor gets exposure for its product/company/business/service/cause by emblazoning its logo and name on the team's jersey, by associating with a healthy, active, team-oriented sport, and by supporting athletes in their pursuit of excellence.

Sponsorship means different things at different levels. At the top professional level, it's a carefully planned strategy laid out by professional marketing companies using scientific research methods to determine target demographics and reach corporate objectives.

Not too long ago, a popular automobile company (named for a planet with rings around it) sponsored a pro cycling team and even incorporated the team and the sport's inherent teamwork into its corporate philosophy. Its sponsorship was not just another public relations arm of its business but became an integral part of the corporate community. It made team members into ambassadors. Saturn riders wore a jersey emblazoned with the corporate logo and spoke intelligently about the automobiles in the Saturn line. The riders knew the history and internal structure of the company, and they had shaken hands with the workers on the assembly line in Spring Hill, Tennessee. They also happened to be excellent riders who would do nothing but train, race, live, and breathe bike racing. They frequently won, too.

Members of the Saturn cycling team were provided with coaches, managers, mechanics, and soigneurs as well as bikes, clothing, equipment, equipment trucks, passenger cars, and an expense account. As if that weren't enough, riders on the Saturn team (as well as other top professional teams) were paid a salary in addition to any prize money they won during the season. It is possible to make a living at bike racing, but paid positions like these are few, and competition for those positions is fierce.

BEHOLD, the Beautiful Swan

"Soigneur" (pronounced swan-YOOR) is a French word meaning to treat or to care for. In 2005, *USA Today* ranked it as the ninth-worst job in America.

Space does not permit me to list all the jobs of a soigneur. And by space, I mean outer space. The unsung hero of the pro cycling world is a massage therapist, launderer, baggage handler, cook, nurse, counselor, office manager, van driver, life coach, psychotherapist, and quite literally bottle washer. Picture Radar O'Reilly, Ugly Betty, and Marge Simpson rolled into one.

Warning: In the amateur ranks, these jobs usually fall on the friend, wife, significant other, or family member.

Aside from racing their bikes, the only other obligation riders have is to make an occasional public appearance on behalf of their sponsor. Saturn riders, for example, frequently conducted "fun rides" at Saturn retailers throughout the country in conjunction with cycling events. This is a good example of a smart sponsor using its relationship with a sports property to bring people into the store. Cyclists and cycling fans would participate in a "fun ride" for the opportunity to ride with professional bike racers. If they should happen to browse the showroom, that would be okay, too.

For the Saturn riders, it was a small price to pay for the ability to concentrate on riding their bikes without worrying where their next meal was coming from. They focused on training and racing in a regimented program with few distractions.

Saturn used riders as spokespersons and cycling as a corporate philosophy throughout its relationship with the team, and it became a model for cycling sponsorship nationwide. It is what most teams aspire to become; it is the sponsor-team relationship that most riders dream of. Just because it was a model, however, doesn't mean that it has become the standard.

VICIOUS CYCLING

In this sport of ours, there is a second tier at the professional level that blurs into the top level of amateur racing. A number of teams have as much talent as the top pro teams but for various reasons haven't been able to attract top-flight sponsors. The vicious cycle begins here. Unable to attract a generous sponsor, riders may be forced to subsidize their income by working part-time jobs during the season and "real jobs" during the off-season. A job, of course, takes a big chunk out of their training regimen, which then prevents them from reaching the highest level of ability, which prevents them from achieving decent race results, which in turn prevents them from attracting better sponsorships. Yet these racers will compete against the top professional riders in 95 percent of the races they enter.

If these riders can somehow break out of the vicious cycle, they may reach the top level, get noticed by the right people, and garner an invitation to join one of the top professional teams. That's the dream that holds young riders in cycling's grasp. Just as aspiring baseball players hope to wear the famed Yankee pinstripes or Dodger blue, talented Roadies dream of one day pulling on the jersey of a top professional team. To do that, though, they need time to train. They also need supportive friends and family. And just for good measure, they also need things like desire, fortitude, ambition, and a strong belief in themselves. The only thing a sponsor can provide is time to train, a highly valuable commodity.

Many second-tier professionals and top-level amateurs actually live a day-to-day existence. There always seems to be a looming threat that their sponsors may come to their senses and realize that they should be supporting a bass fisherman or a skateboarder instead of a cycling team. Many stories can be told of sponsors pulling their funding without warning. It has happened countless times, which has cyclists living a skittish lifestyle, never knowing when the rug will be pulled out from under their feet. And that's when the economy is humming along smoothly. When the economy is struggling, I'd be surprised if any of those riders can sleep through the night.

Additionally, second-tier sponsors are usually smaller companies that don't have large marketing budgets. For example, a small team from the Midwest was sponsored by LDM Technologies, an automotive parts manufacturer, and a bike shop called Kinetic Systems. The team had several great riders but a small budget. It traveled across the United States to compete in all of the major events but had little in the way of support personnel or technical support. Team members only had uniforms, bikes, some cash, and ambition, but they were strong riders who knew how to race.

Planes, Training, and Automobiles

With their smaller budgets, the secondary teams must live frugally. When a top-flight team like Saturn travels, members pack their bikes into nicely padded cases,

SAME Destination, DIFFERENT Routes

It's possible that the Saturns and the LDMs will compete in a race in Miami on June 1 and in another race in Seattle on June 8. How they get from one race to the other is a different story. After the race in Miami, the Saturn riders will fly home, sleep in their own beds, spend the week in familiar surroundings, follow their regular training regimen, and board a plane for Seattle on Friday afternoon. Meanwhile, the LDM–Kinetic Systems riders will spend the better part of the week cooped up in a car on the expressway dodging orange construction barrels and eating at fast-food restaurants. They will stop along the way and ride their bikes each day because a Roadie can't go more than a day without training. To stay on schedule, they will drive beyond the point of exhaustion as they try to get to Seattle in time. They will do their best to arrive ready to race, but they won't be nearly as fresh as their counterparts picking up their bikes at baggage claim.

fly to their destination, and stay in decent hotels that offer HBO, indoor plumbing, continental breakfasts, and clean linen. When a smaller team such as LDM–Kinetic Systems travels, it must stretch its finances in creative ways by driving to its destination with riders' bikes on the roof rack catching every bug, raindrop, rock, or tire fragment the road has to offer. They stay at no-name motels just off the beaten path. Riders cut costs by sharing motel rooms with other cycling teams or staying with relatives. They eat a steady diet of Taco Bell.

These second-tier teams will spend the entire summer on the road, living the vagabond's life traipsing back and forth across the country going from bike race to bike race and living out of their suitcases, eating poorly, and sharing the road with eighteen-wheelers. Eventually, usually in the middle of August, they will reach a point when they're absolutely sick of living this way, and they will splurge on a really nice hotel and a really nice restaurant and blow their entire budget for the rest of the season in one weekend, but it will be worth it.

When the season ends, they will immediately begin looking for more sponsorship for next season. Actually, a better word might be "scrounging." In most cases, riders will have to take at least a part-time job to pay for the extravagant lifestyle to which they've grown accustomed: food and shelter.

A Turn of a Friendly Wrench

Teams at this level are likely to be provided with free bicycles and free equipment. They will not, however, have a mechanic to tend to their bikes between races. For this reason, their bikes will bear the brunt of a long, grueling season on the road.

THE FOOD CHAIN HAS MANY LINKS

Moving below the secondary tier on cycling's food chain, you find a hodgepodge of sponsorship activity. There are a kazillion amateur teams at all levels of ability whose sponsors provide everything from a case of product to a full complement of clothing and equipment.

There are teams that receive the full ride: clothing, equipment, entry fees, travel stipends, and so on. There are teams that have their entry fees paid for

DUCK, DUCK, LOOSE

There was once a team called Team Duckhead sponsored by the well-known clothing company. The team included several really good riders who enjoyed tremendous success for a couple of years in the early 1990s.

Team Duckhead came to my hometown for a weeklong series of races in August, and I had an opportunity to spend some time with the riders. Aside from their tendency to eat, sleep, and live as cheaply as possible, I noticed that every one of their bicycles was on the verge of collapse. One rider's bike had at least eight things wrong with it: The big chainring was bent; the bottom bracket was cobbled; the headset was shot; both wheels were out of true; the rear derailleur wouldn't get up to the two smallest gears; the rear tire had a slow air leak; and the chain skipped.

This was the bike belonging to someone who raced his bicycle for a living. In Chapter 2, I wrote, "On a racing bike, everything works."

I lied.

---

the entire season; they'll have to pay the rest of their expenses out of their own pockets (or out of the pockets of friends and family). There are teams that receive free hotel rooms. This makes it a lot cheaper to travel to races out of town.

There are teams that receive a lump-sum payment from their sponsor at the beginning of the year and never hear from the sponsor again. You would be surprised to learn how often this is the case.

CHARLES IN CHARGE

The process of acquiring sponsorship at this level isn't easy. These teams won't produce the same results as the professional teams, nor will they enjoy a great reach into the market, making them a tough sell to prospective sponsors.

At this level, the process of acquiring sponsorship usually begins with one proactive member of the club/team who takes the initiative to write a letter. Several people will offer suggestions as to what that letter should contain, but usually one person drafts it. It will be sent to one, two, or several local businesses and will contain a proposal for sponsorship that includes some explanation about the sport. There will be a list of the benefits of sponsoring a cycling team and, most importantly, a request for money.

If the letter is successful in attracting a sponsor, everyone on the team will celebrate. If it's not successful, everyone on the team will blame the person who wrote it.

LAST BUT NOT LEAST

At the bottom of the food chain, we find the bike-shop teams, who receive nothing more than a 10 percent discount on bike parts at a local bike shop. They'll start out by getting a bunch of guys together and calling themselves a team and hopefully coaxing a bike shop into printing its name on their jersey in exchange for a discount on bike stuff. That might be all they get for sponsorship, but it can add up to a lot over the course of a season. It doesn't really cost the bike shop anything to offer this benefit; in turn, it gets exposure at bike races, its target audience.

Attitude is everything, and even the smallest cycling teams will do their best to take on the appearance of a professional team. The general belief among Roadies is that any sort of sponsorship serves to validate their formation, so they take great pride in designing their custom jerseys, and they will try to act as ambassadors for their sponsors no matter how small their sponsorship may be.

QUICK-CHANGE ARTISTS

If you spend any time in the sport, you will likely observe one of the problems associated with the sponsorship of amateur teams and clubs: uniforms. Getting everyone outfitted with the same clothing is expensive. First, let's review the clothing needs of a typical club rider with the approximate costs:

2 short-sleeve jerseys @ $40 = $80
2 bib shorts @ $65 = $130
1 skinsuit @ $70
1 long-sleeve jersey @ $65
1 jacket @ $80
1 vest @ $40
3 pairs of socks @ $15 = $45
TOTAL: $480

Now let's multiply $480 by the twenty club members who intend to race next summer. The total price for new clothing is $9,600. There aren't many sponsors who will shell out that kind of dough to sponsor a local cycling team. Instead, each rider will be paying for his own clothes out of his own pocket.

At the end of the season, teams will go through the entire process again. They hope to retain the same sponsor. If they change sponsors, they'll have to redesign their clothing to reflect the change. Sometimes the changes are minor and affect only the printing on the uniform. But sometimes the changes aren't so subtle. For example, if the twenty-member Acme Cycling Club receives $4,000 in sponsorship from the local Red Roof Inn, the riders will probably wear red uniforms to reflect the sponsor's corporate color. If Red Roof Inn drops its sponsorship and John Deere lawnmowers (green and yellow) provides the $4,000 sponsorship for the next year, a complete change will result. As we just saw, however, $4,000 won't cover the cost of new uniforms.

LOOK AT IT THIS WAY

The Chicago White Sox have changed the design of their baseball uniform more than any other professional sports franchise. How would the team look if individual players were allowed to wear any version they wanted?

Would they look like a team? Or would they look like a walking advertisement for a vintage clothing store on Sunset Boulevard?

Cyclists who belong to a sponsored team might have to buy a new set of clothes each season in order to represent their team and sponsor properly. A problem arises when some members buy the redesigned clothes while other members can't afford to. Some riders show up at the races wearing the new green-and-yellow clothing while others wear last year's red edition.

Do you see what can happen? A club can have several riders in one race calling themselves one team, but they may be wearing three or four different jerseys that the club has acquired over the past few seasons. That's confusing to the other racers, the spectators, and the announcer who is trying to explain what's going on. We can toss the word "uniform" out the window.

YOU LOOK MARVELOUS, BUT DO YOU RIDE MARVELOUSLY?

Talk of sponsorship and how it makes riders look and feel like professional teams means little when the race is under way. No amount of colorful advertising printed on a jersey can replace hours and hours of training. For professional and top-level amateur teams, we've seen how sponsorship can help riders dedicate themselves to

the sport, but on the local and regional levels, sponsorship is emphasized too often as a necessary aspect of team development when in actuality the roadside of cycling is littered with teams that looked great but couldn't ride fast or didn't know how to ride as a team. And that's what it all boils down to. Like four guys who grab some guitars and call themselves a band, if they can't make decent music, nobody will want to hear them play.

Learning to ride as a team means

- Knowing the subtle strategies that can be employed
- Knowing the strengths and weaknesses of every teammate
- Being able to change strategies during the race
- Reacting to other teams' strategies by adapting one's own
- Working together without having to say more than a few words
- Making a commitment to each other to train hard and work on the essential skills
- Sacrificing one's own desire and opportunity to succeed to help a teammate win

Many Roadies will tell you that being a good team rider means packing your ego in a small cardboard box and burying it in an unmarked grave in your backyard. When it works, teamwork is the coolest thing in the entire sport, whether you have a sponsor's logo on your jersey or not.

PEANUTS

Though we long for the day when sponsors flock to our sport in droves, we know it is our lot in life to work hard for little reward. We've come to accept it, and we don't allow ourselves to get upset at the disparity between our sport and others. There is, among Roadies, a widespread acceptance of the fact that every one of us is racing for peanuts compared to other sports. Let me give you two examples.

Example 1

The purse for the PGA Championship is $6.5 million, of which the winner takes home $1 million. The winner walked four rounds of eighteen holes but didn't have to carry his own clubs. The entire purse for the U.S. Pro Cycling championship is

$250,000, of which the winner takes home $50,000. He rode 120 miles and can hardly walk up to the podium to accept his check.

Example 2

I participated in a bike race in Bay City, Michigan. The winner of my race received $125 for two solid hours of intense bike racing in miserably hot, humid weather. I finished in third place and received $75 for my trouble.

After the race, I was sitting in my car trying to muster the energy to change out of my cycling clothes. I heard a distant PA announcer's voice emanating from Bay City's riverfront a few blocks away. Curious, I got out of my car and ambled toward the sound. When I got close enough, I could hear that the announcer was conducting the awards ceremony for a bass-fishing tournament that had just finished. (Ironically, it was sponsored by Shimano.)

My jaw dropped when I heard the prizes. The eighth-place fisherman—the guy who caught the eighth-largest fish of the day, the guy who sat on the shady riverbank for two hours and wiggled a lure in the Saginaw River while I tore my legs off for $75, the guy who appeared to have never missed a barbecue in his life—received a cash prize of $230. I almost fainted. I couldn't bear to wait around to find out what the third-place finisher received. He probably won a shiny gold Mercedes and a date with a movie star.

FINAL LAP

Getting back to the story that introduced this chapter, for the record, Miller Lite isn't "the right beer now." Coors Light is. Or at least it was in July 1993.

Let's move on.

PART FOUR
RIDERS READY

12. The Criterium

I was only eight years old when I first felt the hook of cycling, but because I lived in a remote country town where a combine was a farm implement, not a race tactic, it wasn't until I was sixteen that I attended my first bike race.

It was the strangest thing I had ever seen. My American sports mind couldn't make much sense of it. The race was held on city streets in a downtown area on a short rectangular course encompassing about two city blocks. The race was fifty laps in length. The first forty-nine laps seemed to be a game called "Try-to-Guess-Who's-Winning." The final lap was the only thing I understood because that was when the riders really got busy.

It was a form of mayhem, and I kind of liked it. The colors, the shapes, the speed, the danger, and the foreignness of it all made quite an impression on me.

OH, SO THAT'S WHAT IT WAS

I later discovered that the type of race I witnessed that day—several laps around a short course—is called a criterium. It's a purely American style of racing that is the bread and butter of bike racing in the United States. "Criterium" is similar to a French word meaning "competition," but in France the race is called a *kermesse,* which is a Flemish word. The British, who have a funny name for everything, call this race a "roundy-round" due to the fact that riders essentially ride 'round and 'round.

In the United States, a criterium (or "crit") is a race held on a short course consisting of many laps. Were I a more sarcastic person, I might describe it as "a multilap race on a course with many dangerous turns held on a Sunday with no spectators in sight." But I'm never sarcastic.

These races are very fast, often dangerous, and short enough to suit the American attention span. And because the riders complete each lap in about a minute, a criterium is thought to be spectator friendly. This is in contrast to the long-distance road race that lasts for hours and is nearly impossible to watch from the sidelines. At a crit, the crowd can see what's happening as the race unfolds before them.

A COURSE IS A COURSE, OF COURSE OF COURSE

When you go to a football game, you know what the field of play is going to look like. It will be 100 yards long, flat, and green with funky poles located at either end. There are no surprises. The same can be said for a basketball court or a hockey rink. Bowling alleys, wrestling mats, volleyball courts, tennis courts, snooker tables, and ping-pong tables are of a standard size. Aside from the depth of the outfield fences, even baseball fields have standard measurements. And though each venue has its own quirks and personality, all of them fall within the measurements prescribed in the rulebooks.

As you may have guessed, Roadies have no idea what a racecourse is going to look like until they arrive on race day.

The shapes and designs of bike racecourses vary greatly. The USCF has no rules governing the shape of a criterium course. As long as it's reasonably safe, the USCF will allow the race to proceed. The chief referee may require that hay bales or barricades be placed around areas of concern (light poles, fire hydrants, and other immovable objects) to protect riders and spectators. For the most part, though, the responsibility for safety falls on the riders, who are required to sign waivers releasing the promoter from liability.

The most common shape for a crit course is square with four 90-degree corners. The most common length is between 0.6 and 0.8 mile. Experienced Roadies have seen many variations and have their own opinions about each one.

The start/finish line is usually located on the longest straightaway. This is due to a USCF rule requiring that it be located at least 200 meters past the final turn (where feasible). This is a good rule to observe because the final sprint is dangerous enough when it's in a straight line. To add the danger of a corner to the mix would be mayhem.

Although cyclists complain about the course design, every racecourse produces a winner—the racer who negotiates the course faster than anyone else. Despite complaints about a tricky or challenging course, somewhere in that field there will be a rider who figures out how to survive the race and win it. What makes the crit most challenging is its corners. If you can't get through a corner quickly and safely, you will not enjoy much success in this type of bike race.

LET'S GET THIS PARTY STARTED

As noted in Chapter 10, an announcer invites all racers to the start line. This usually initiates a mad scramble for position as riders attempt to start as close to the front of the group as possible. I'll explain why this can be important in a moment.

At larger events, there may be a ceremony that includes playing the national anthem. There may be official starters, a few remarks by the sponsor, and special introductions of notable riders. This is our one chance to give special recognition to current and former national champions and other riders of note by bringing them to the front so that spectators can see them clearly. If done correctly, introductions add a special element to the event. Unfortunately, this places the top riders on the front line in the perfect position. Any rider who isn't given a special introduction (90 percent of the field) must scramble for a decent starting position behind the stars.

As riders stand at the starting line awaiting the green light, they must adhere to a simple rule that states that every rider must be standing with at least one foot on the ground when the starter's pistol is fired. Obviously this rule prevents any rider from taking a flying start. As a result, all riders will have one foot on the ground and one foot engaged in the pedal in anticipation of the start of the race.

At the sound of the gun, there is an awkward lurch forward as the riders push off from a complete standstill. They must get the bike rolling and then quickly engage their foot. You'll hear a very cool sound during the first moments: a cacophony of clicks as 100 shoes are engaged into their pedal. This is followed by a burst of speed as everyone scrambles to get going.

FALSE STARTS

Don't be alarmed if you see the riders begin to roll forward before the starter's pistol is fired. In fact, they may roll several feet beyond the start line before hearing the gun blast. This is perfectly normal and acceptable. There isn't a race referee on earth who will stop the race and conduct a restart. It really doesn't matter. As long as no one leaps away at a tremendous speed, no one is going to get upset about this.

Don't be alarmed if you see some riders tangle and tumble in the first few pedal strokes of the race. Because they're so tightly packed into the starting area, they may hook handlebars. It's usually more comical than harmful. Since they're moving so slowly, injuries seldom occur. The real risks here are embarrassment and broken equipment. That's not comical.

TOE CLIPS

In the old days, the start of a race had a different sound. Cyclists once used metal toe clips with leather straps to affix their feet to the pedals. It would take Roadies a few pedal strokes to wrangle the pedal into position so as to wiggle their foot into the toe clip and tighten the strap. In those first few pedal strokes, the metal clips would scrape on the pavement, producing a wretched screech. With the advent of clipless pedals, the wonderfully horrible sound of 100 metal toe clips scraping across the pavement vanished from the cycling scene.

HOLD ON TIGHT

We're off and running. Though this race may look like a fast-moving parade that's stuck on a perpetual loop, it's actually an ever-changing body with many different events taking place simultaneously.

The first lap of a criterium is chaotic. The fight for position begins immediately after the gun is fired. Riders who didn't have a decent starting position will try to claim a spot at the front as quickly as possible. Riders who did have a decent starting position will try to hold on to their spot. In the meantime, riders will be initiating their strategies immediately. These three efforts drive the pace of the race up.

Pre-race jitters usually linger into the first few laps of the race. This also drives up the speed. Old-timers used to say that the first five laps of a criterium are the fastest. The fact is that all laps are fast. The first five are just really, really fast.

Eventually the race settles down and finds its own rhythm. The first few laps will be very busy for the riders. Subsequent laps won't be slower, but they will be less frantic.

If the course is particularly challenging or dangerous, riders will place great importance on having a decent starting position. This will guarantee the mad scramble described earlier.

ALL IS QUIET ON THE WESTERN FRONT

A rider hoping for success needs to be at the front of the pack, where the attacks take place and breakaways form. A rider at the back will miss them. Also, those at the back of the field will be of no help to their team should their teammates get in a breakaway.

The specter of crashing motivates most riders to fight to hold a position near the front. Fewer crashes occur there. The farther back in the pack you ride, the better your chances of being involved in or caught behind a crash. The three or four seconds that it takes to either pick yourself up off the ground or squeeze past a melee of fallen riders might be enough to take you out of contention as the rest of the field rides away. The group will never stop to wait for you.

CORNERING THE MARKET

Remember that a criterium is held on a course that contains many corners, much like a Grand Prix auto race. It's the corners that give the criterium its special charm.

Mathematically, the most efficient line to ride through a turn is a smooth, continuous arc rounding off the corner as much as possible. Does this mean there's only one possible line through a turn? Of course not, but a smooth arc allows for the highest speed to be maintained from Point A to Point B. In theory, any other line through that turn will be less efficient, and therefore slower.

A single rider negotiating a corner has the freedom to select the very best line through the turn, avoiding potholes, manhole covers, cracks, and so on. One, two, or a handful of riders can negotiate it without significant loss of speed if they are in a single-file line. When you have a hundred bike racers riding through a 90-degree turn together, riders must adjust to one another. Consequently, the field will slow.

When you watch a hundred riders squeeze through a tight

turn, you can understand why this is such a high-risk area. Multiply that risk by the number of corners on a course and the number of laps, and that will explain why a criterium is not an event for meek, timid, or delicately nurtured individuals.

TURN OF A FRIENDLY CARD

If you envision a breakaway taking place on a straight road, then you're going to have to make some modifications when you apply it to the criterium. The corners play an integral role in the breakaway scenario because they can disrupt the rhythm and slow the peloton.

You already know that a single rider or small group can go through a corner very quickly. The only way the peloton can move through the corner at the same speed as a small group is to do so single file. Anything wider than single file will have to traverse the corner at a slower speed.

That's a key point. We're only talking about a difference in speed of a mile per hour or so, but that equates to time, and time adds up.

YOU'RE A BLOCKHEAD, CHARLIE BROWN!

We're going to use blocking to buy more time for a breakaway led by George. As noted in Chapter 6, blocking can be active or passive. In a criterium, one or two riders can control the speed of the peloton if they know how to use the corners to their advantage. With George in the breakaway, we will position ourselves at the front of the field as it goes through a corner; we only have to slow down a little and force everyone behind us to slow down as well. Now, getting from Point A to Point B may take 5.25 seconds instead of 4.25. That's an extra second per corner, or four more seconds per lap!

Slowing in the corner where it's nearly impossible for anyone to pass is as active as blocking can get. Each time we create a logjam, we put space between our group and George's breakaway group. Yes, it's legal. As long as we don't do it in a danger-ous manner, we can do this through every corner on the course.

OUT OF SIGHT, OUT OF MIND

Another aspect that corners add to the criterium is the phenomenon that Roadies call "out of sight, out of mind." Once the breakaway puts a couple of corners be-tween itself and the field, the field may forget about the leaders.

a MATH EXAMPLE

As George's small breakaway zooms through a turn at a steady speed of 28 mph, it takes the riders 3.5 seconds to get from Point A to Point B. Meanwhile, the large peloton will find it rather cumbersome to get through the turn. In fact, it may take riders 4.25 seconds to cover the same distance because they have to mesh together and avoid running into each other.

Big deal, right? You bet it is! It means that the field will lose .75 second per corner. Multiply that by four corners per lap, and the math tells us that the riders face a deficit of three full seconds per lap. Theoretically, according to this simple example, the breakaway can increase its lead by thirty seconds after ten short laps of the course.

Can you guess what's coming next?

No, I'm not kidding. It's crazy but true. It's not guaranteed that once a breakaway is out of sight, those riders will stay away for the win. It's just something I've seen happen many times, especially on tight courses with many corners and limited sight lines.

If the field forgets about the breakaway, it will be reminded when the breakaway comes up from behind and "laps the field."

THE CASE OF THE LAPPED FIELD

It's not uncommon for a breakaway to gain a lap. When the leaders' strength is combined with the efforts of their teammates who are blocking, it's quite common indeed, especially on a short course. It is an occurrence that changes the complexion of a race. Suddenly some new dynamics emerge:

- The breakaway's cooperative agreement becomes null and void. There is no longer a need to work together.
- Breakaway riders will try to lose their breakaway companions in the pack, and if they can, they will break away again without them, thus further improving their odds of winning.
- Teammates will endeavor to position their leader near the front and be on guard for attacks by breakaway riders of opposing teams.
- The breakaway riders will zoom through the field like grubs through my front lawn and immediately push the pace of the race again.

TONIGHT'S DINNER: PRIME RIB

Here's another term to throw into the criterium mix: "prime." First of all, we pronounce it "preem." It's a noun. The exact origin of the word is disputed among cycling historians. For our purposes, where it came from doesn't really matter. All that matters is that you know how to pronounce it, how to use it, what it means, and what it does to the criterium.

A prime is an unscheduled intermediate prize that's given to riders during the race at the discretion of the promoter, officials, or announcer, or by some other means. It is given to the first rider to cross the finish line on a particular lap. It's a feature that is added to the race to make it more interesting by creating more sprinting.

Here's how it works. As the field passes through the start/finish area, a bell is rung and the race announcer declares the prize. One lap later, the first rider to cross the finish line is declared the prime winner. In essence, it is a single-lap race within a race.

The prize is usually cash but can be anything. When I was a race announcer, I gave away a lot of money. I also gave away a lot of gift certificates and merchandise. At one race, I gave away a decorative lamp and a coffee table. At the Frigidaire Classic, I gave away a refrigerator and a microwave oven to two riders. (Karen Bliss and her teammate, Sue Yeaton, to be exact!) These may sound like odd prizes, but Roadies have come to expect things like that, especially when the race is sponsored by, say, a furniture store or an appliance manufacturer. That's bike racing!

The cool thing about a prime is that no one knows when it will happen. Since riders never know when the prime bell is going to ring, teams have no chance to organize a lead-out. When the prime bell rings and the prize is stated by the announcer, all a rider can do is assess the situation and decide if he wants to sprint for it. It's purely optional.

PEEKING AT THE CARDS IN OTHER PEOPLE'S HANDS

Another benefit of the prime is that it reveals the fast, aggressive riders to both the crowd and the other riders. After two or three prime sprints, everyone in the field (that is, anyone who is paying attention) knows who is strong and therefore likely to be a contender in the final sprint.

A warning to spectators: Don't be misled. Sometimes a rider will avoid the primes and wait for the final sprint to come out of hiding. For the entire race, we may hear the same five or six names mentioned by the announcer throughout the race in prime sprints, breakaway attempts, solo attacks, and so on. But if, in the final sprint, we hear the announcer call out the name of a rider we've never seen before,

BRUBAKER

The rider who lurks in the pack until the end and then emerges to win the race is similar to Robert Redford's character in the 1979 movie *Brubaker*. Redford played a warden newly assigned to a prison in need of reform. Rather than enter through the front door, he disguises himself as a prisoner and spends the first few days checking out the scene through the eyes of an inmate. Nobody knows he is the new warden—not even the prison staff.

Then one day, deep in the bowels of the prison cleaning out solitary-confinement cells, he steps forward and says, "I'm Brubaker. I'm your new warden." Now, you have to admit, there aren't too many situations in real life like that one, but I think the situation I just described comes pretty close. A rider pretending to be just another piece of field fodder waits for the perfect moment to step forward and say, "I'm Brubaker. I'm your race winner."

Of course, when Robert Redford appeared dressed in prisoner fatigues early in the film, everyone in the theater could predict what was going to happen.

then we know that this guy stayed quiet throughout the race with one goal in mind. He patiently waited, overcoming the temptation to make some easy money while everyone else sprinted for the primes. He kept his ego in check while he checked out all the angles. When the time was right, he emerged.

Another result of the prime sprint is that it sharpens the skills of the officials. With each intermediate sprint, they have a chance to prepare for the final sprint, in which the big money is on the line. They can test the photofinish camera. They can work out any bugs that might occur. Let me remind you that we build a race venue each time from the ground up. That means that the officials must set up their equipment and test it to make certain it works. The prime allows them a chance to work out the bugs.

A LULL IN THE ACTION

Races are not fast all the time, and the speed can fluctuate wildly. Sometimes the riders look like they're not even racing at all. The race will go as fast as it wants to go when it wants to go. There will be lulls between the furious attacks. By comparison, though, the lulls can look like a Saturday in the park. I think it was the Fourth of July.

Just wait a few minutes. Every period of calm is followed by a storm.

WHEN BAD THINGS HAPPEN TO GOOD ROADIES

By this time, you may have had a disturbing thought: With so much happening in a criterium, what if a rider has a crash or a flat tire? Is there some rule that allows him to recover from the mishap and continue the race?

Since fate plays a big role in a bike race, a provision has been written into the rules to protect a rider who suffers a mishap or a mechanical failure. The reason for this is simple: The success of a rider should not hinge totally on the fickle finger of fate. A flat tire should not be the cause of anyone's demise, nor should a crash bring someone's day to a premature end. And since a rider who suffers a mishap would immediately fall out of contention, we have a solution.

The promoter is responsible for providing a service area somewhere along the course, usually a wide spot in the road near the start/finish area. We call this area the wheel pit. It contains spare wheels, spare parts, and a mechanic who knows how to fix bikes in a hurry. It also contains a race official armed with some quick judgment.

When a rider is involved in a "mishap" (crash) or a "mechanical failure" (the bike breaks), he will report immediately to the pit, if he is able. He will assess the damages, fix what needs to be fixed, and jump back into the race. However, the amount of time from the moment the rider crashes to the moment he is released back into the race could be in excess of a minute! In that amount of time, the peloton could have completed a full lap, which means that our rider is now a full lap behind the leaders.

This is where the solution comes into play. It's called the free lap rule, and it allows any rider who has suffered a mishap to remain in the pit area for one complete lap while his bike is repaired. This allows him to retain his position in the race. When he is released into the race, he will be placed in the same group he was in prior to the mishap.

Here's a stipulation: The free lap rule applies only to an act of fate. If the rider has a mechanical failure, the official determines whether that failure stems from improper maintenance or fate. If it was indeed an act of fate, the rider is placed back in the race when the peloton passes by. However, if the failure was due to faulty maintenance, the rider will be placed back into the race without the benefit of a free lap and will be required to make up any lost time on his own.

Some examples of mechanical failures caused by fate are flat tires, a broken chain, a broken spoke, or a cracked frame. Some examples of faulty maintenance include a poorly adjusted derailleur, loose parts, failing brakes, or a slipping seat post. The responsibility for those falls directly on the shoulders of the Roadie. Therefore, no free lap!

FORT PIT

The wheel pit is another element of the sport that varies greatly from race to race depending on the budget of the race. At the big events, tech support is provided by a component manufacturer (Mavic, Shimano, Campagnolo, SRAM.) that staffs and outfits the pit with everything from spare wheels to spare brake cables. These people come equipped with tools of every shape and size, capable of fixing anything that breaks. They also provide professionally trained, uniformed mechanics who can fix almost anything in less than a minute. If a rider rolls into the pit with something that can't be fixed immediately, the mechanic will provide the rider with a fully equipped loaner bike for the rest of the race.

When a tech support crew provides all of the equipment for a race, it is required to provide services to all competitors equally: "neutral support." At small and medium-sized events, the wheel pit operates a bit differently. Instead of a neutral support mechanic providing spare wheels and parts, each rider is responsible for supplying his own wheels and parts.

Earlier I told you about placing a simple means of identification on the Roadie's spare wheels. This is where those wheels will be located during the race. If there is a mechanic on duty, his services are neutral, but the Roadie must supply his own equipment. Instead of calling this a neutral wheel pit, we refer to it as a "wheel in–wheel out."

Often, though, the pit is just a collection of wheels thrown in a roughly organized pile. A Roadie will be on his own to find his own parts and fix his bike.

THE BIKE IS FINE, BUT THE BODY ISN'T

Race promoters are required to provide emergency medical services. Placement of the ambulance is left to the discretion of the promoter. Often the EMT crew will take up a position that allows it access to a main thoroughfare to facilitate a quick response elsewhere if needed. In many cases, the promoter will position the EMTs where they will expect to attract the most business: near the most dangerous corner on the course. Either way, it's a good idea to be familiar with the location in advance. Bike racers and their families need to know the location of the nearest hospital, what insurance coverage they have, and how to handle dire consequences should a crash occur.

HAVING WHAT IT TAKES

What skills must a Roadie possess to achieve success in a criterium? You may have already guessed that he needs nerves of steel, excellent bike-handling skills, the ability to endure fast and repeated acceleration, and the ability to throw a plan out the window and wing it at any time. It helps to have a handful of dedicated teammates working on your behalf, but that's not always the way a criterium is won.

Some Roadies don't enjoy criterium races. They hate the crashes, the rapid speed changes, the shorter distances. Some riders simply detest the format altogether. This is unfortunate, since most racing in the United States is done on a criterium course.

If you were to select the perfect bike for this, it would be light, stiff, and nimble. It would be very responsive to your need for speed because in a criterium the speed is constantly changing. It should be nimble because you're going to move it through corners very quickly.

HOW TO RIDE A CRITERIUM

Keeping in mind the danger that lurks in every corner, the best way to ride a criterium is to stay near the front of the field. Avoid the temptation to drift to the back because moving up through the field is difficult when the field is constantly winding through corners. Be prepared for a lot of sprinting as the speeds change constantly.

I can't overemphasize the need to practice the art of cornering. If cornering becomes second nature to you, you can focus on breakaways and other tactics. If not, you will be tentative through every turn while everyone else is zooming past you. It's no fun to race your bike when you're scared to tears.

Remember, the "out of sight, out of mind" phenomenon can work for you or against you, depending on how you look at it.

HOW TO WATCH A CRITERIUM

Where should a spectator stand to watch a crit? At your first race, your senses may be so overloaded that it won't really matter where you stand to watch the race. It will all look the same no matter how you look at it. You will likely be unable to tell one rider from the next. Eventually, over time, it starts to make sense. When it does, I urge spectators to watch the first few laps of the race from a location near the start/finish line. Then take a leisurely walk around the course and watch the race from various angles. There's not a race in America that prevents spectators from roaming around the entire course with the freedom to stand inches from the action. This freedom is one of the cool things about bike racing that I hope never changes.

I enjoy watching the faces of first-time spectators as the field zips past them at 30-plus mph. They feel the full force of the wind that the field kicks up as it passes, and their faces light up with shock as it literally takes their breath away. Also, the idea that so many riders can ride so closely together and so fast is bewildering.

Should you go to a criterium or take a first-timer, it's important to always consider the safety of the riders as well as your own personal safety. Hold on tight to young kids, and be ready to jump back should a crash occur.

The bigger bike race events will likely have some sort of fencing around the course to prevent spectators from wandering into the street. They may also have a sound system that projects the entire length of the course so that the announcer's commentary can be heard everywhere. A sound system like this will let you stand wherever you want for the finish of the race and still be able to hear the outcome.

The smaller events will likely provide sound coverage only on the home stretch. Really small events probably won't have an announcer or a sound system, so as a spectator you'll be on your own to keep track of the laps and everything else.

As I mentioned earlier, there's no perfect place to stand to watch the finish of the race, and you may not see the critical point of the race. Over time, you will decide what's important to watch and what can be missed without regret.

A ROSE BY ANY OTHER FORMAT

In case the criterium becomes dull, the promoter has a few options to spice things up. By tweaking some of the rules, there are a few creative ways to select a winner. I'll give you a brief description of some of the favorite variations on the criterium race. Ask any Roadie to provide further details and war stories.

Format 1: Devil Take the Hindmost

Also known as the "miss and out." On every other lap, the last rider to cross the finish line gets pulled from the race. This continues until there is only one rider left. Crazy, huh? Think of it as musical chairs on bikes.

Format 2: Win and Out

This is the opposite of the miss and out. In this variation, several sprints take place. The first sprint determines the winner and only the winner. The winner is immediately out of the race. Done. Finished. You win; you're out. Thanks for coming. Your work is done here. Subsequent laps determine subsequent placings.

Format 3: The Points Race

The points race is a normal criterium peppered with intermediate sprints held every five laps. Points are awarded to the top three riders in each sprint. The final sprint is worth double points. Whoever accumulates the most points wins. Get the calculator ready; this race is a spreadsheet waiting to happen.

Format 4: Street Sprints

Some people don't have the patience to watch an entire race. These are the same people who skip ahead to the last page of a mystery novel to find out whodunit. For these folks, bike race promoters have brought drag racing to cycling in the form of street sprints, or straight-line sprints.

To start this event, riders are held upright on their bikes at the starting line by impartial volunteers. Riders are held motionless with the front tip of their front wheel aligned with the starting line. They should be fully engaged in their pedals and ready to pounce. A USCF official will give the signal to start with a preparatory command of "riders ready" followed by a whistle or gun.

Distances range from 200 meters to 500 meters, and the outcome of each heat tends to be decided by mere inches; there is seldom a runaway winner. There is never a breakaway. There's no time for team tactics. It's simply a display of brute strength, top speeds, and the occasional crash. Due to the nature of the event, it attracts only the sprinters or riders who think they can sprint. Few nonsprinters are willing to show their inability to the general public in this forum. For them, it would be easier to simply carry a sign that reads, "I have no fast-twitch muscles in my legs!"

Here a false start is of critical concern. We're only racing 200 meters. We can't allow any riders to have a head start.

For this event to run properly, the persons holding each rider upright at the starting line must be totally impartial. All they do is stand behind the bike and hold on to the saddle until the whistle blows. Then they simply let go of the bike. The rider will take it from there. The holders do not assist the rider in any way.

Have I ever seen someone cheat during a straight-line sprint event? Only once, but that is a story we can skip.

PICKING AND CHOOSING

All information regarding the format of a particular race is published in the race flyer so that every cyclist knows what to expect. No rider wants to spend five hours in a car driving to a race only to discover that a different race format is being presented. Although racers love to race their bikes, not every racer loves to race a win and out or a points race.

Don't worry about keeping these formats straight. The chances of you seeing anything but a plain ol' criterium are becoming increasingly slim as the other formats are slowly fading into obscurity. I'm not crazy about this trend, but I'm powerless to stop it.

FINAL LAP

Although Roadies love to race their bikes, most would prefer to avoid the criterium format. Many riders believe the criterium is too much of a crapshoot or a matter of being in the right place at the right time. It's not always the strongest rider who wins, much to the chagrin of the strongest rider.

For the Roadies who don't particularly enjoy riding a criterium, there is the road race. It requires a chapter all its own.

13. The Road Race

When I mention bike racing, few people envision the criterium. Instead, they probably conjure up an image of a large group of racers out on the open road racing over hill and dale. That's the road race!

A road race usually covers between 50 and 120 miles. It is often held on country roads far from civilization. The route can be from Town A to Town B, or it can be of the out-and-back variety. It can be made up of one huge loop or several laps of a long loop. It can be hilly or it can be as flat as a skillet. We are all at the mercy of the race promoter.

Obviously, with a course that traverses up to 120 miles, it's impossible to close the roads completely to vehicular traffic as we do in a criterium. Only in some truly rare instances, such as the national championships, is it possible to create and maintain a total road closure. Instead, we use a partial closure to keep motor vehicle traffic from interfering with the race, and vice versa.

THIS IS DEFINITELY NOT A CRITERIUM

The pre-race mood at a road race is laid-back. I can give you a few reasons for this.

First, the start of a road race is far less frantic than the start of a go-from-the-gun criterium. Second, the risk of crashing in a road race is considerably lower. This

takes away a lot of the pre-race anxiety. Finally, road races tend to be grueling. If you know the next four hours are going to be a death march, you won't be too anxious to get started.

Riders congregate at the start line at the appointed time. Here in the road race, good starting position is not so critical. In fact, it's not uncommon for riders to miss the actual start of the race because they were busy fishing arm warmers out of their car or searching for a coffee shop. No worries.

It takes a different kind of rider to master the road race. If a criterium is a melding of brute strength, split-second decision-making, chance taking, bike-handling skills, and good old-fashioned luck, then a road race is a combination of strength, endurance, brains, patience, and a high tolerance for pain.

Strength is needed to go fast when necessary. Endurance is needed to ride fast for a long time without fading. Brains are needed to play the rolling chess game. (There is no escaping the fact that every race involves the brain.) Patience is needed to fend off the temptation to react to every little thing that happens. And finally, a high tolerance for pain is needed because a long, grueling road race hurts. A lot.

I CHOSE THE ROAD LESS LEVEL

You may recall from the previous chapter that a criterium is held on a short course with many corners that directly affect the race. In a road race, the tricky turns are replaced by challenging terrain and longer distances. Does this make the road race easier than a criterium? Some Roadies may say so. But there are other elements that make road racing much harder. For many, it's the hills.

In many road races, the ability to climb becomes equal to or greater than the ability to sprint. A hilly road race will supply its own selection process; those who can get up and over the hills faster will find success. Those who cannot, will not.

It's that simple. A course with several big hills will whittle away the pretenders until the true champion emerges. In fact, many people feel that a true road race-course must include challenging hills.

There is no rule governing the terrain. Every aspect of course design is left to the discretion of the race promoter.

PROFILING

The key things for a rider to know are the course map and the course profile. The map is obvious. The course profile is a graphic representation of the terrain that illustrates where the hills are located.

In a criterium, riders have a chance to study the course in advance of the race. It involves a short walk around the block. With a road race, riders may get a chance to ride it in advance of the race or drive the course to look at the hills, curves, and final miles. At the very least, they should take a look at the major hills and the last couple of miles to inspect the approach to the finish. A Roadie doesn't want to be surprised by what's around the next corner.

My point is simple. You need to know the important features of a road racecourse if you're going to entertain thoughts of winning the race. Smart riders actually tape a copy of the profile and some mileage notes to their handlebars for quick reference. Teams also use radio systems to stay in contact with their team directors, who can advise them of upcoming situations.

SURPRISE!

In the 1985 Coors Classic, Davis Phinney was in a three-man breakaway with Bernard Hinault and Steven Speaks, preparing to sprint for victory in the town of Truckee, California. As they rolled into town, Phinney spotted a banner hanging across the road that looked like the finish-line banner, so he started sprinting. With relative ease, he won the sprint to the banner. Unfortunately, the banner that he thought marked the finish line was actually advertising a rodeo that was coming to town the following weekend! Yeehaw!

"Yeehaw" is exactly what Bernard Hinault said as he sprinted past Phinney to the real finish line and the real victory that came 100 yards farther down the road.

THE RACE CARAVAN

The team director is located in the race caravan. The caravan consists of several vehicles that follow the peloton through the entire race. It is a parade unlike any you've ever seen. It varies in size according to the size of the event. At major road races, it will include twenty or thirty vehicles performing a variety of functions:

- Officials watching the race for rule adherence
- Team directors providing tactical and technical support to their riders
- Mechanics who have the entire wheel pit loaded into their cars
- Photographers and journalists providing media coverage

- Motorcyclists providing a safe escort
- Police protecting both the public and the race entourage

The casual observer would be astounded by the level of activity in the caravan. Cars and cyclists maneuver about as team managers and mechanics attempt to service their respective riders. Photographers zoom about trying to get the best angle on the action. Officials orchestrate the entire thing as it winds its way over hill and dale at an average speed of 25 mph. If you've ever seen bicycle messengers weaving through rush-hour traffic in Manhattan, then you have a sense of what life is like in a caravan.

Were it not for the fact that most law enforcement agencies turn a blind eye to what takes place in the caravan, cycling would never see another road race.

All major bike race events include a caravan of twenty to thirty cars and several support personnel. At the other end of the spectrum, in smaller events the caravan may be scaled back to include only (I'm not kidding here, folks!) a lead car in front of the field and a pickup truck chock-full o' wheels behind the field. That's the extent of it.

Either way, the riders remain oblivious to it all. They focus on one thing: the race.

TRAFFIC CONTROLS

Now is a good time for me to explain the concept of the rolling enclosure. Simply put, a rolling enclosure is like a Canadian funeral procession. In Canada, provincial law once required all drivers to pull over and stop when a funeral procession approached. Motorists were permitted to resume driving only when the last car in the procession had passed. (Nowadays, the law only requires drivers to slow to half the speed limit.) Okay, that's probably not the best analogy, but you get the picture, don't you? Instead of closing the entire road racecourse to traffic, we only stop traffic for the time it takes for the race to pass.

To perform a rolling enclosure, we place a few vehicles in front of the race at enough distance to warn oncoming motorists of what's approaching. In many cases, a sheriff's patrol car is the first vehicle. Sometimes a local motorcycle club is recruited as "moto-marshals" to provide this service. To be effective, these marshals should communicate to oncoming motorists by use of hand gestures to slow down and move to the side of the road.

Motorists who are aware of the chaos that's coming their way will wait alongside the road until the group of cyclists passes. Whatever they decide to do after the race passes is not a concern of ours.

Motorists who approach the race from the rear are blocked by a well-marked follow vehicle. They have to be patient and follow along at 25 mph until we part ways. Every now and then, an impatient driver gets fed up and tries to pass the entire race on a two-lane road. I've seen it happen. It is one of the scariest moments in life. There's not much a race promoter can do to prevent this from happening aside from placing a sheriff's patrol car in that position as a deterrent to such behavior.

The rolling enclosure becomes quite a feat when the field is divided into many groups. For example, imagine a breakaway that holds a lead of eight minutes over a chase group and another five minutes over the main field. Do we hold traffic for almost thirteen minutes? Is it even possible to hold traffic? Do we have enough escorts to cover three groups? What if the field breaks up even further? How many intersections does the race pass through? How many driveways does it block?

Blazing through intersections, screaming over freeway overpasses, and wending its way across the countryside at an average speed of 25 mph, the locally promoted road race operates on a wing and a prayer and regularly peers over the edge of disaster.

So to recap what I've just explained, the rolling enclosure provides a safe envelope for the racers while allowing the minimum disruption to traffic patterns. This system is used at most larger races. Smaller events do not use a rolling enclosure.

The roads remain open. All riders adhere to a USCF rule that prohibits them from crossing the yellow center line of the roadway. It's referred to as the yellow-line rule, and though it's widely respected, it's problematic to enforce. And a ribbon of paint offers little protection from oncooming traffic.

Significant risks are involved in conducting a race on an open highway. Roadies involved in the race often become blind to the dangers of road racing. The discussion in this chapter should give you some idea of why criteriums are so popular in the United States. They're much easier to manage.

IF IT LOOKS, SMELLS, AND SOUNDS LIKE A ROAD RACE . . .

The design of the course is left to the discretion of the promoter who must provide for the logistics involved with the course marshals, road closures, law enforcement assistance, and safety. As I mentioned at the beginning of this chapter, the road racecourse can be set up in a number of ways.

Point-to-Point

To put it simply, the start of the race is at Point A, and the finish is 120 miles away at Point B. Logistically, it is the most challenging design. It requires building and staffing separate starting-line and finish-line venues. Among other concerns, it requires transporting equipment and resources from Point A to Point B.

The Loop

It's much easier to get permission to use and manage twenty miles of road six times than it is to manage 120 miles of road once, so the most common road racecourse design is a ten- to twenty-mile loop that is repeated several times. Instead of separate start and finish venues, there is one venue that does both jobs. Fewer jurisdictions are involved, which makes it easier to hold the race. The racing is generally the same, but the logistics are more manageable.

Circuit Race

The circuit race is a variation of the loop that provides the elements of a road race but is easier to manage. This race is held on a course that is about two or three miles in length. The course is normally closed to traffic or held in areas where traffic is regulated, such as a park or industrial complex. I've seen circuit races held at the famous Laguna Seca Raceway in California, the only slightly less famous Road

FROGGER REVISITED

In order to observe a road race, your objective is to get to various points on the course without driving on the course itself. The traffic flow on the course will be clogged because of the race. You must do everything in your power to avoid getting caught in traffic.

Before the race begins, you plot the racecourse on a map and select your viewing areas (waypoints) along the route. Next, you plot a secondary route you will follow to the various waypoints.

Immediately after watching the start of the race, run to your car and drive directly to the first waypoint. Get out. Wait and watch as the peloton blazes past. Yell words of encouragement to your favorite rider. Make sure he hears you. Get back in the car and drive to the next waypoint, using your secondary route.

Repeat this as many times as possible before the finish of the race. Leave yourself plenty of time to get to the finish area, park, and get a good viewing spot for the finale. Remember, the race ends in a flourish that lasts mere seconds. If you waste any time, you will miss it.

Always remember: He who travels light travels fast. The more people you take with you, the more likely you are to be delayed by someone having to use the restroom.

Always obey the posted speed limits and laws of the land. You will not see the finish of the race if you are locked up in a county jail. Trust me on this.

America in Wisconsin, and the Chrysler automotive test track in Michigan. Roadies like a route that's completely closed to traffic. It relieves them of one source of angst.

HOW TO WATCH A ROAD RACE

From a spectator's standpoint, the road race is challenging to watch, and the point-to-point is the most difficult. Compare this to a baseball game at a major league ballpark where everyone sits in assigned seats from the opening pitch to the final out. In a point-to-point road race, if spectators wish to watch the race from beginning to end, they have two choices: They can rent a helicopter, or they can play leapfrog. Since helicopters rent for about $300 per hour, most people opt for leapfrog. Leapfrogging a bike race can be a lot of fun with a large group of people, but it's logistically easier with two or three people per car. The whole thing is exciting in its

THE CLOCK IS RUNNING

While leapfrogging the Tour DuPont as it traveled through North Carolina in 1995, some friends of mine made a quick pit stop at a convenience store to restock their provisions. They thought they had plenty of time to pick up drinks, chips, and Kit Kat bars. The entire pit stop probably felt like it took thirty seconds when in fact it took eight minutes. (Such is the effect of distorted time.)

Unaware of this, they reached their next waypoint and stood alongside the road for several minutes joking and eating and having fun. Hey, the bike race should be coming by soon! Party on! Slowly the realization came over them that they had missed the peloton. Their eight-minute pit stop should have been a three-minute pit stop. Their suspicions were confirmed when the broom wagon passed their location.

At large events such as the Tour de Georgia or the Amgen Tour of California, the broom wagon is always the last vehicle in the caravan. It can be identified by the brooms attached to its bumper. The brooms symbolize the clean sweep this vehicle makes of the course. Any rider who drops out of the race will be picked up by the broom wagon and carried in silence to the finish line. If you see this vehicle, you have seen the end of the race.

own road-rally type of way, though it may be asking a lot of spectators to go to such lengths to watch the race.

Always remember that seconds count when you're proceeding from one waypoint to the next. You may feel as though you have plenty of time to dawdle, but you don't. Time becomes twisted and distorted.

HOW NOT TO WATCH A ROAD RACE

Less dedicated spectators watch the start of a race and then go to the shopping mall for three or four hours, making it back in time to catch the finish. That's how my friends do it when they come to watch me race. When I get back to the car after having spent the last six hours getting my butt whooped, they say, "Great job, man!" as they try to hide the shopping bags filling the car.

So we have leapfroggers on one end of the scale and mall rats on the other. Halfway between those extremes are friends who attend the race and camp out at the start/finish area, spending their day sunbathing, reading, napping, and listening to the announcer. There's nothing wrong with this method of bike race spectatorship.

If the announcer is good and is providing a steady flow of information, it can be very exciting in a radio-drama kind of way.

Whatever level of involvement a spectator chooses, it's free of charge. That's one very cool thing about cycling that will never change.

Someday, when pigs fly, American road races will be broadcast live on network television, using three helicopters to follow the action from start to finish. Until that day, we will have to lug our lawn chairs and coolers and magazines out to the side of the road to see the excitement. For now, I hope you have a better idea of what to expect.

DON'T GO to the Mall

As a rider, it's heartening to know that someone is going to great lengths to play leapfrog in order to see us race. To see the same people at several different spots along the route is a cool thing. It means they're interested to see the race and know what's going on.

FINAL LAP

The road race is the most grueling of all race formats. It requires more strength and endurance than any other sport I can think of—with the possible exception of the Ironman triathlon. To understand the brutality of a road race, consider this: Someone who plays an entire game of soccer will run back and forth on a flat surface for four fifteen-minute periods with plenty of rest time between each period. In ice hockey, players will be substituted constantly over three twenty-minute periods. In baseball, they will sit in the dugout for half of the game. Although these games are physically demanding, the duration is rather short, and there are built-in rest periods.

In a road race, riders spend between three and seven hours in constant competition. There is seldom a chance to collect your thoughts, let alone rest your body. It is a mental drain as much as a physical drain. By the end of the race, a Roadie will experience the depths of exhaustion: soaked in sweat, covered with road grime, unable to walk upright, tired beyond comprehension, and hungry enough to eat a horse. That's bike racing!

Ask any Roadie—it's the most awesome feeling in the world.

14. The Individual Time Trial

If, for some bizarre reason, a rider doesn't like to race in the criterium or the road race, the USCF offers the time trial. For a long time, I hated time trials. I love them when they're exciting, but I hated them the other 97 percent of the time. I love watching the exciting ones, but I hated racing in any of them. If that becomes evident, then I apologize in advance to all those Roadies and fans who love and adore time trial events. I have learned to love them. Okay, that's a little strong. I like them.

Many Roadies enjoy a love-hate relationship with the time trial. Those who like to ride it love it. Those who don't, really don't. It offers an entirely different aspect of racing, one that's more mathematical and calculated and much less influenced by luck. It is much more personal. It also requires an entirely separate collection of equipment.

The reason some riders hate the time trial is simple: It's hard. There is no place to hide in a time trial. There is no synergy. It's one rider alone, a true test of his ability to ride fast and suffer without the benefit of knowing where his competition is or how anyone else is doing. A time trial is essentially the same as walking cold into a final exam: You will find out how much you know based on how much you studied. No cheating. No copying.

ELEGANTLY SIMPLE

The individual time trial (also referred to as simply "time trial" or "TT") is a simple format for determining the fastest rider. It is specifically called the individual time trial because each individual rides a given distance alone. Whoever has the lowest time for completing the course wins. There isn't much strategy to speak of. When the pedal comes up, push it down. Repeat as necessary. It's that simple. But of course I have more to say about it.

The key word to reflect on is "alone." The time trial is a solitary race against the clock, but it's also a race against oneself. Wind, gravity, and friction are physical elements that each rider must overcome, but the real battle takes place inside the rider's mind.

This is a race that takes strength, endurance, efficient technique, a high threshold for pain, and incredible concentration. The best time trialists have the rare ability to disconnect the thoughts of the mind from the actions of the body. This allows them to ignore the pain for long periods and ignore any self-defeating thoughts that creep into their minds. If a rider can't overcome those negative thoughts, it really becomes pointless to race in a time trial.

Obviously the struggle between the racer's mind and body is invisible to the spectator. For this reason, the time trial can be dull from a spectator's point of view. There isn't much to see: just an occasional rider going really fast.

THREE . . . TWO . . . ONE . . . GO!

A time trial begins in a less exciting way than mass start events do. There is no ceremony. There is no starter's pistol. In fact, if you aren't looking for it, you may not even know the event has begun.

At most events, an area is set up near the starting line for bike inspections. Officials need to determine whether a bike conforms with the multitude of specifications set out in the rulebook. As technology has advanced, riders have found new ways to slip through the wind. Rules have been implemented to prevent anyone from gaining an unfair advantage. The bike inspection area is where riders will report after checking in at the registration tent.

Riders start their race individually at one-minute intervals assigned to them upon registering for the event. The responsibility rests with each rider to know his assigned start time and be ready to go when that time comes. Woe to the rider who arrives late, for the clock starts to run at the scheduled time whether he is on his

We call the starting line a "start house" because at the major events like the Tour de France, there is a small structure (about the size of Mickey Mouse's camper) that sits on a platform raised about three feet above the road surface. It has stairs at one end, allowing riders to enter the start house, and a ramp out the other end, allowing riders to get a rolling start.

At many smaller events, the start house is a 10-by-10-foot pop-up tent situated next to the starting line.

In 90 percent of all time trials in the United States, the start house is nothing more than two officials holding clipboards, eating bagels, and drinking coffee next to a piece of duct tape stuck on the road perpendicular to the traffic lines. This is where the riders depart on their solo journey.

It really doesn't matter what the start house looks like because each rider spends only fifty seconds of his day there.

bike or elsewhere. (Ask any Roadie to tell you the story of a Spanish racer named Pedro Delgado. In July 1989, he elevated himself to patron saint of missed start times.) Approximately one minute prior to his scheduled departure, a rider will officially report to the starting line, or, as we call it, the "start house."

When a rider is ushered into the start house, he is placed on his bike at the starting line and is physically held upright by the starter's assistant. He has both feet fully engaged in the pedals and both hands on the handlebars. As the clock approaches his starting time, the official counts down the final five seconds. When the clock reaches zero, the rider starts his race. Immediately after one rider leaves, the next rider rolls up to the start house, and the procedure starts again.

The lack of fanfare surrounding the start tends to create an air of ho-hum around the entire event. There is little visual excitement at a time trial. All there is to see is a bunch of individual riders coming and going at a high rate of speed. For that reason alone, this event is not regarded as spectator friendly. Venturing out onto the course while the race is under way won't bring any more excitement to a spectator; there's simply not a lot to see.

ON THE ROAD AGAIN

The time trial course generally ranges from four to twenty-five miles in distance. There's probably a secret formula a promoter uses to determine the exact length of a time trial, but I'm guessing it mostly has to do with the availability of manageable roads. As in the criterium and the road race, the promoter's ability to obtain permission to use the roads often determines where the race will go. Though a promoter may have every intention of running the race on a lightly traveled, scenic stretch of twisting, curving pavement on rolling hills along a babbling brook under the shady canopy of stately oak trees, the harsh reality is that he will run the race on whichever road the local authorities allow. Most often this means a terribly boring stretch of pothole-riddled pavement through an undesirable part of town, or through farmland located out beyond the airport.

In most cases, the time trial is held on a roadway that is open to public traffic, thus giving the full responsibility of safety to the riders. That single factor makes the logistics of a time trial far easier than that of the road race or the criterium.

SMALL, MEDIUM, AND LARGE

A time trial can be held on a point-to-point course or a loop course, but the most common type of time trial course is out-and-back.

At most time trial events, the entire process of setting up an out-and-back course is to simply paint a line on the road, wave a magic wand, and declare it the start/finish line. Somewhere down the road, an orange traffic cone has been placed in the middle of the road and denotes the turnaround point. With the exception of a tree-climbing competition, I can't think of many sports that require so little in the way of venue construction and preparation. The only way you can tell a race is happening is that cyclists are milling about. The emphasis is clearly on the results of the race rather than the presentation of the event.

Only for major events will the entire road be closed, controlled, and protected by law enforcement agencies from start to finish. At these major events, you will also see a more elaborate production with huge clocks and scoreboards, Daktronics video walls, and food vendors. Don't expect to see Daktronics video walls at too many cycling events.

CLOCK WATCHERS UNITE

As I mentioned, the time trial is a personal battle between each individual rider and the ticking clock. Because the clock reigns supreme in this race, the USCF officials whose job it is to keep track of all the numbers become ad hoc accountants. Let's take a moment to show respect for those individuals who selflessly give their time so that riders may partake in such an interesting event. These people are not thanked nearly enough.

Let me give you an idea of why the USCF officials are worthy of our admiration. If George's starting time is 9:33 a.m. and he crosses the finish line at 10:07.39 a.m., then we can do the math and determine that his total time is 34:39. If Jason's starting time is 9:36 a.m. and he crosses the line at 10:10.37 a.m., then we do the math again and see that his total time is 34:37. Jason beat George by two-hundredths of a second. That sounds pretty easy to compute. Here's one for you to try:

> Rider 1 starts at 8:25 a.m. and finishes at 9:14.28 a.m. for a time of _____.
> Rider 2 starts at 8:33 a.m. and finishes at 9:21.15 a.m. for a time of _____.

That was simple. You probably didn't need to use a calculator. Now, let's multiply it by the 450 riders who are signed up to race in this event covering all categories, all age groups, and both genders, starting at 8:00 a.m. and running until 4:00 p.m. Rain or shine.

If you enjoy this sort of thing, the USCF is looking for people like you.

By the way, by my calculations, Rider 2 finished with a time of 48:15. Rider 1 was 1:13 slower.

RACING THE RACE

Once under way, a racer only needs to ride fast and avoid crashing into things. That may sound simple, but the one thing that makes the time trial such an intriguing event is the one thing that heightens the danger: concentration. A rider who is so sharply focused on riding can become blind to the most obvious things. For example, curves in the road.

Many of the worst cycling crashes occur in the time trial event when Roadies mistakenly ride with their heads down in an effort to get into the best aerodynamic position possible. Since these bikes are built purely for speed and not for handling, things can go haywire quite easily.

FANCY-SHMANCY BIKES

Speaking of bikes, I haven't properly acknowledged the many important advances in bike technology. In Chapter 2, I glibly said that "the bicycle has not changed much in the past fifty years." Well, I didn't want to get too complicated, but now I'm ready to reverse my position.

Indeed, the technology of the sport has changed dramatically in the past ten years. Bike frames are now made of all different types of materials with an eye toward achieving greater efficiency. Frame designs and their geometry have changed to allow different riding positions to be explored and exploited. Riding positions continue to change as new ways to slip through the wind are discovered and more efficiency is milked from the pedaling motion while adhering to the strict rules set forth by various governing bodies. For example, wheel designs have gone through a number of changes. They're still round, but that's about the only thing that has remained the same. The use of carbon fiber and fewer spokes has made them much lighter, stronger, and more aerodynamic. High-tech clothing has gained a few seconds per mile. Training methods have resulted in a rider who is almost a moving computer full of data on every body function. It has been a race to make the bike as efficient as possible to generate as much speed as possible when there is a rider on its saddle.

But if everyone has the latest equipment with the latest technological developments, then we're back to where we started. It must be the intangibles that help a rider win a race like the time trial: desire, determination, discipline, resolve, training methods, and a belief in oneself.

Spectators aren't able to see those intangibles. For spectators to get any enjoyment out of watching a time trial, they must understand that there's a war going on inside every rider, and not every rider has the natural ability to ride fast. Some riders have the ability to go fast, but they lack concentration and the discipline to follow through in a race situation. Knowing this, it becomes more interesting when you see the second-place rider finishing just one-tenth of a second behind the winner. Spectators are left to wonder what small thing made the difference between first and second places. Riders are left to discover ways to increase their speed and reduce their time.

One more pedal stroke might have made the difference. A better riding position might have made the difference; possibly a more efficient turnaround at the halfway point or a better breakfast. A cleaner bike? Freshly shaved legs? One less piece of pizza? One more hour of sleep? When a race can be won by a tenth of a second, every little thing matters. To many, that is the allure of the time trial.

Knowing this, you can imagine that Roadies who are serious about the time

trial get picky about the bike they're riding. If they can shave a second here and a microsecond there, they will. In fact, they will go to astounding lengths to make their bike more efficient.

To many, this is the true allure of the time trial: to tweak a bike in order to gain a slight advantage, be it from the aerodynamics, the gearing, the efficiency of the pedal stroke, the position of the rider, the weight of the bike, or any other aspect. A Roadie will stay up all night fine-tuning his time trial bike.

FANCY-SHMANCY SOUNDS

Bike racing produces some cool sounds, but none quite as interesting as a time trial bike passing by at high speed. A carbon-fiber disc wheel with a super-inflated tire makes a distinctive scratchy, resonant sound that is hard to imitate. It means one thing to a Roadie: speed . . . and pain. Okay, two things.

But he might do better to tweak his riding technique, training methods, and fitness levels because, as noted earlier, the USCF imposes some fairly strict rules regarding the bike and how much it can be modified to slip through the wind.

HOW TO WATCH IT

If you're going to watch your Roadie ride a time trial, I suggest that you go to the starting line and watch him take off. Start your own stopwatch when he begins so that you can keep track of his time. Hop in the car. Drive to a particularly challenging part of the course. Wait for him to come by. Yell as many words of encouragement as you can in the short time that you see him. Drive back to the start/finish area and wait for his arrival.

While you're waiting for him to return, you may be able to ascertain the current "time to beat." At smaller events, this may be impossible, and in fact, it's best not to disturb the officials. They have their hands full with the task of collecting and transcribing the data. At medium-sized events, the announcer should be able to provide that information to the crowd.

At major races, the information is displayed in real time on scoreboard clocks. This is when a time trial is an exciting event to watch. When you can see the incoming rider's time side by side with the current leader's time, the payoff is immediate. These events can be heart-stoppingly exciting. In the absence of these data presented in real time, however, the time trial remains a very personal experience that is difficult to share with spectators. As a result, when your Roadie crosses the finish line, you should stop your stopwatch. Meanwhile, he'll probably continue riding for a few minutes to cool down. When he returns to his car, you'll be waiting with a fresh bottle of water, an encouraging word, and an accurate but unofficial reading of his time.

TAKING SOME FRIENDS ALONG FOR THE RIDE

A variation of the individual time trial is the team time trial (TTT). It's not much different from the individual time trial except that the team event is conducted with four-man teams. Remember how synergy works in the paceline? That same principle is hard at work in the team time trial. Consequently, the speeds are usually higher; in addition, the distances are usually longer.

The team race starts in the same manner as the individual time trial: Teammates are held upright by starter assistants at the starting line. The clock starts when the official says go. But since there are four riders, the clock stops to record their time a little differently: when the leading edge of the front tire of the third rider crosses the finish line. Read that line again if you have to. It's a bit confusing. USCF rules state that three of the four riders must finish the race, and to guarantee this, the official time is taken on the third rider, specifically, the leading edge of the front wheel.

All of the same characteristics apply regarding excitement, inner struggle, and intense concentration. As an added bonus, since we have four riders working to-gether, chemistry is a major factor. The ability to rotate the paceline without dis-ruption of rhythm is essential; four riders must work together as one from start to finish. No longer is it a race of solitude and inner reflection. It is a bigger focus that encompasses the individual as well as the whole.

You may have already guessed that additional riders bring the risk of collisions. When one of the four riders goes awry, he can take all three companions to the pave-ment in a heap.

You may think that the team time trial is more fun because there are three other people to talk to while speeding across the landscape. Unfortunately, no one talks during this event except for one or two words at a time. Usually, all that is heard is the loud, rhythmic, labored breathing of four riders working at 95 percent output. That's one of the cool things about it. The really good teams are the ones who ride in silence.

FINAL LAP

Ah, yes, the time trial. Cycling's version of the bank statement. The race that anyone can try. All you need is a bike, a course, and a stopwatch. I would also suggest clothing, however tempting it might be to eliminate drag altogether. I mean, let's not lose our heads here. There's no sense ending up in jail for indecent exposure.

15. The Stage Race

I'm not much for camping. Oh sure, I'll sleep in a rest area on the freeway in Missouri on my way to a bike race in Texas, but cycling leaves little time for real camping. During a rare real camping trip a few years ago, I woke up early and rolled out of my sleeping bag. I climbed out of my tent and stood up on the fifty-yard line of the Super Bowl. (This may sound like a dream sequence, but stay with me; it is a true occurrence.) I found myself standing elbow to elbow with about 120,000 insane fans from around the world. People with orange body paint were dancing and singing a song I can't even begin to imitate. There were food vendors and souvenir booths everywhere I looked. Flags from more countries than I ever studied in school were hanging from the trees and road signs. People were painting gigantic words all over the ground, and nobody bothered to stop them.

Obviously it wasn't really the Super Bowl, nor was it the infield at a NASCAR race—it was something much larger: the biggest party in the sporting world, lasting all day and well into the night. On the next day, we did the whole thing again with many of the same people on a new road in a new town. And the reason we slept in tents, cars, or motor homes or on park benches at night and stood out in the hot sun all day long was to wait for the Tour de France to pass by. We scouted out what we had decided was the best location in the French Alps to catch literally a glimpse of the greatest sporting event in the world, and we simply camped out there until it came to us. That's how it's done: Pitch a tent alongside a mountain road and wait. A sore back and no sleep are your ticket into the stadium.

Every sport has its pinnacle, and this is ours. The Tour is often compared to the Super Bowl, which is ironic because our entire view of the actual race lasted almost as long as a Super Bowl television commercial. Comparing the two events is really a case of apples and oranges; they are as different as night and day. To us, the Super Bowl is like a third grader's birthday party while the Tour de France is like a royal coronation.

If the casual observer has any exposure to the sport of cycling, it's most likely through the Tour de France. The Tour operates in the stage race format, which we seldom see at the amateur level in the United States. Still, since the Tour is our Wimbledon, Masters, Indy 500, and World Cup rolled into one, I feel that it's necessary for you to have a basic working knowledge of the stage race format. I will also try to explain the major tours and why we hold them in such high regard.

BACK IN THE SADDLE AGAIN . . . AND AGAIN . . . AND AGAIN

Simply stated, a stage race is a multiday, multirace event in which each day's race (called a stage) is timed and, more importantly, each rider (or group of riders) is timed individually. The winner is determined by the lowest cumulative time.

If I beat you by a margin of ten seconds on Day 1, you will have to beat me by eleven seconds on Day 2 to take over the lead. If you are able to do that, we will give you a specially colored jersey to wear so that everyone can identify you as the new race leader. If you are unable to beat me by eleven seconds, I will continue to wear the leader's jersey.

Although the format may be simple, the stage race is a true test of endurance and strength, a monumental logistical feat, and a complex web of strategy and tactics over the course of 100 to 2,100 miles.

Stage races range in length from three days to twenty-three days and are usually made up of road races and time trials. Take everything you already know about the grueling nature of a single bike race with its complex team tactics and mental exercises and add several days of back-to-back racing, and you'll begin to understand what makes the Tour de France and other stage races special.

Each day offers its own excitement as an individual race. There is great emphasis on, and prestige in, winning an individual stage of any stage race. However, the

drawn-out nature of the stage race creates more mind games and chess moves that contribute to making it more interesting—and more difficult to actually win.

Let's not think that because we're racing on consecutive days, we'll be holding back each day to save some energy for tomorrow. No. Each stage is raced at full throttle. That's a remarkable feat when you consider how difficult this sport is. When you take into account how much recovery is needed after a single race, stringing several races together back to back puts even more emphasis on strength and endurance.

GC: THE MATH OF RACING

Since there are almost 200 competitors in the race, each day offers an opportunity for someone to take the leader's jersey away from you. In each race, you must keep track of who is attacking. You need to know how much of a margin they had over you at the start of the race and how much of a margin they have over you during the race. That's not confusing, is it?

Of course it is. And it's easy to imagine each rider carrying a notebook full of spreadsheets attached to his handlebars.

Each day, the current standings are posted for all riders to see. But we don't call them the current standings. No, this is bike racing, where we have an unusual name for practically everything, and we call it the GC, which stands for general classification. It provides a complete list of names (and teams) of everyone in the race placed in respective race order, and it provides the amount of time separating each rider from the lead. Riders study this information each night between races. They memorize the names (and race numbers) of riders they'll need to watch in the next day's race.

THE KEYS TO SUCCESS

What's cool about the stage race is that you can win one day's stage and lose the next, but what matters in the end is the bottom line. Because this race is based on math, it's possible for a rider to win the entire shebang without winning a single stage. Think of it this way: Miss Michigan doesn't have to win the swimsuit competition, evening-gown competition, talent competition, or interview in order to receive the Miss America crown. She just has to finish among the leaders in each one.

It's also possible to win five out of six races, but if you lose that sixth race by a big margin, you can lose the whole shebang. Your hold on the leader's jersey is so tenuous that one bad day can ruin you. If Miss Ohio wins the swimsuit, evening-gown, and talent competitions but totally bombs the interview, guess who won't get the tiara and the bouquet of roses?

In stage racing, you have to be like a military general because the whole war is made up of smaller battles. The best weapon a Roadie can have in his arsenal is consistency. If you know that having one bad day can ruin your chances, then you need to find a way to deliver the same strong performance on each stage. This requires a solid understanding of your physical limits and abilities.

If you should ever find yourself wearing the leader's jersey, you and your team-mates will rest uneasy knowing that everyone else in the race is gunning for you. You're wearing a big bull's-eye on your back with that leader's jersey. That makes you easy to find, and everyone is looking for your weak spot. They're waiting for you to falter. They'll have time to think about ways to make you crack over the course of multiple days, as opposed to having one shot at you in one race, as with a single-day event. As soon as the day's race ends, you must begin preparing for tomorrow's race in every single thing you do, from the food you put in your mouth to the pillow you rest your head on. (Valuable advice: Don't go to the dance club, museum, aquarium, shopping mall, or zoo.)

Conversely, if you are one of the challengers hoping to capture the flag from the enemy, you will lie awake at night thinking of all the possible tactics and what-ifs. You'll look for any way to gain a slight advantage over your competition.

Self-confidence is essential. Roadies who suffer from self-doubt will want to choose another career.

THE MYSTIQUE OF THE DOMESTIQUE

When a contender rolls up to the starting line on the first day of a stage race, he brings with him a well-rounded team. Just as in football, where there are specialized positions with well-defined roles, a cycling team has riders who will forfeit their own chances of success in support of their team leader. They will carry out their assign-ments during the race with the diligence of soldiers. They may never win a race in their careers but instead allow themselves to be used as pawns in a chess game.

The most interesting of these positions is known as a "domestique." Like the nameless football lineman, this rider will go to the depths of the ocean to help his team leader (also known as the GC contender) stay fresh and in contention, whether that means retrieving food, water bottles, or spare clothing from the team car or setting the pace at the front of the race. He may give his bike to the leader in the event of a flat tire. (Rather than wait for the service support car to respond, which could take several seconds or minutes, the domestique will simply trade bikes with the team leader, give him a push to get him going, and then stand on the roadside holding a flat tire and a bike and wait for help.)

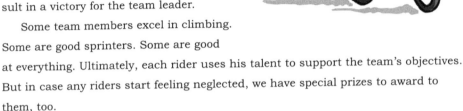

It's not a thankless job. The domestiques are handsomely rewarded for their efforts, especially when those efforts result in a victory for the team leader.

Some team members excel in climbing. Some are good sprinters. Some are good at everything. Ultimately, each rider uses his talent to support the team's objectives. But in case any riders start feeling neglected, we have special prizes to award to them, too.

KOM AND FRIENDS

In addition to the pageant winner, Miss USA offers prizes to other contestants: Miss Congeniality and Miss Photogenic. These winners are voted in by delegates and Internet respondents, respectively.

In cycling, we have a different way to select winners of secondary titles. The King of the Mountains (KOM) competition awards points to the first four riders who make it to the top of selected climbs. Customarily, the first rider over the top receives five points. Second place gets three points. Third place receives two points. Fourth place receives one point. Each day, the points are added up, and the rider with the most points is awarded a distinctive jersey marking him as the KOM leader. At the end of the stage race, whoever holds the jersey is declared the winner of that competition.

The Sprint competition awards points to the first four riders to reach designated points along the route. The point system is similar to that for the KOM, with the winner receiving five points, second place receiving three points, etc. Each day, the points are tallied, and the rider with the most sprint points receives a unique and stylish jersey to proclaim his status.

The LONG SOLO BREAKAWAY

At some time while watching the Tour de France, you will see a lone rider in a solo break-away with a lead of twenty-two minutes over the seemingly careless peloton. To the casual observer, the world seems to be spinning off its axis. How could they let this guy get such a big lead?

It happens all the time, and here's why. Since the Tour is televised live from start to fin-ish throughout the world (except in the United States, where it is preempted by coverage of dog shows and rodeos), there is great value in getting your face (and sponsor's logo) onto the TV screen. So the rider you see way out in front for eighty miles of the race is (1) a do-mestique and (2) a four-hour-long television commercial for his sponsor. He has been given the blessing of his team leader to go off the front in search of airtime for the mother ship.

If he should happen to do the unthinkable and actually win the race, his sponsor will be ecstatic at the additional publicity, and his career will benefit greatly. This is why, on the rare occasion that it does happen, the rider is elated beyond tears. It truly is the greatest moment in his life.

The solo victory is unlikely. The peloton will usually plan its chase efforts to slowly reel in any type of breakaway before getting to the finish. But every now and then . . .

Both of these competitions are held while the race is under way. For example, if we're racing from Point A to Point Z, there will be a sprint line at letter J, letter S, and the finish line. Meanwhile, we'll pass over mountains at letters F, M, and X. Consequently, officials will be positioned at those points to record the finishing order and keep track of the sprint points and KOM points.

To be eligible for the Best Young Rider Award, a rider must be under the age of twenty-three (U23). The highest-placing young rider on GC is given a special jersey. A rider may be several minutes behind the leader on GC, but if he's the highest-placed U23, he'll be awarded the jersey.

The Most Aggressive Rider competition is not charted by points or time. Instead, like the Miss Congeniality award, it is voted on by members of the media at the end of each stage. They will look for the rider who is most active at the front of the race throughout the day. The rider who is named Most Aggressive will wear his own spe-cial jersey in the following stage.

There is also a prize given to the best team in the race. This is determined by taking the cumulative times for each team. The lowest time wins. Though tracked in the published GC results after each stage, this award is usually given only at the end of an event. Sadly, there is no special jersey for this prize. No sash. No crown. No flowers. Just the title Team GC winner. A sash would be a nice touch, but it might get caught in the chain of the bike. That would be messy.

All four jerseys carry a certain amount of prestige. In order to win the award at the end of the event, the rider must complete the race. Having enough points to be declared the winner isn't good enough to actually win; you must finish the race.

These competitions are designed to showcase the talents of riders who likely won't contend for the overall victory. There are riders who come to the stage race with no intention of winning the overall title. Instead they will concentrate on winning a particular stage or one of the secondary competitions.

Before we move on, I think you should know that Vermont has provided us with more Miss Congenialities than any other state. That's some useful noncycling information for you. Now, back to my campsite in the French Alps.

THE GRANDEST OF GRAND

I can't explain the giddy excitement I felt when I was setting up my tent. There is an electric buzz that surrounds the Tour de France. Everyone who made the trip to that remote section of road felt the same way. Anyone who looks at the crowd stretching for miles to the horizon can't help getting swept up in the carnival atmosphere.

It's one thing to buy a ticket to, say, a University of Michigan football game and sit in the "big house" with 107,501 fans for a couple of hours. It's an entirely different planet you're on when you trek up a remote mountain in the Alps and watch the Tour. And there are two other tours of only slightly less magnitude.

Tennis and golf each have four grand-slam events during the course of their seasons. Tennis has the U.S. Open, French Open, Australian Open, and Wimbledon. In golf, they play the Masters, U.S. Open, PGA Championship, and British Open. All of those events are well-known to even casual sports fans.

Cycling has three grand tours. These special events each last twenty-three days and are about 2,100 miles long. That's what sets them apart from all others. The three grand tours are held in France, Italy, and Spain. The Tour de France, held in July, is the biggest tour in regard to prestige and importance. The Giro d'Italia in June is considered to be the second fiddle, but by no means easier. The Vuelta a España, held in September, is the third jewel in the crown. Individually, we refer to the three events as the Tour, the Giro (JEE-ro), and the Vuelta (VWEL-ta). If you say those words, Roadies will know instantly what you're talking about. No need to say anything more.

Other professional-level stage races last only a week and cover less ground. Still considered major events on the calendar, they differ from the Tour de France in length and stature, yet they have the same look and feel as the Tour, Giro, and Vuelta. In that respect, they're much like golf tournaments. The PGA has four major tournaments that draw all the best golfers, attract worldwide attention, and carry the most prestige. There are also tournaments of lesser stature, such as the Buick Open and the Memorial. To the casual observer, they look quite similar but lack the circus atmosphere that the major tournaments enjoy. The same can be said of cycling's professional stage races; the major races enjoy more prestige, hype, pomp, and glitz. Some of the more popular weeklong events include the Tour of Britain, the Tour Down Under in Australia, Paris-Nice in France, and Tour de Lankawi in Malaysia.

SENSE OF SCALE

To give you some idea of how large these major stage race events are, they have the clout to shut down twenty miles of major metropolitan motorways during rush hour for a bike race. These big stage races are about the spectacle as much as the results. Therefore, the start/finish area is very elaborate. The race caravan is enormous. And the army of volunteers and staff that supports the event can be several hundred strong. The crew that supports the Tour de France for twenty-three days numbers in the thousands. The fleet of vehicles and tons of equipment required to produce each day's event for both France and California—not to mention the clocklike precision in which they move—would make the U.S. Navy envious. Consequently, when these tours roll into town, they tend to take over the joint quickly.

That's part of the fun, and since it's a positive experience for spectators and communities, the sponsors receive positive attention throughout.

A THIN SLICE OF ECON PIE

In addition to providing an exciting race, a stage race generates an economic impact by attracting visitors to the region. I can present a running marathon that will create excitement in a city for a day. It will have an impact on the local economy. A

ALL THE WORLD'S **A STAGE RACE**

There are a handful of weeklong professional stage races in the United States. California and Georgia each have their own very successful version. Utah, Colorado, and Missouri have joined the scene with their own tours. We'll likely see more stage races crop up as states discover cycling's popularity and marketability because there's more to a stage race than the race itself.

single-day bike race will do the same. A golf tournament lasts four or five days in one corner of town. A tennis tournament may last a week, but it is held in a sports complex designed specifically for tennis. A stage race, on the other hand, has a huge footprint that blankets a region. These events also act as a picture postcard to the rest of the country to promote tourism throughout the year. And if that weren't ambitious enough, some races have a philanthropic component as well. For example, the Tour de Georgia has a goal of raising awareness and funds for the Georgia Cancer Coalition.

The stage race is an important marketing tool for sponsors of all kinds. Each of the special jersey competitions has its own sponsorship, so every photograph of the sprint leader displays the sponsor's logo. Whenever the KOM leader is in a breakaway, TV images of him in his sponsored jersey are beamed around the world to television and Web site viewers. When the Best Young Rider does something special, his image may show up in newspapers around the globe. This commercialism isn't limited to bike racing or NASCAR. Many sports are finding ways to show you a logo or two. Even in the field of music performance, we see logos. Why, after a concert pianist plays a Rachmaninoff concerto, do I feel compelled to run out and buy a Bösendorfer piano? Probably because its logo was staring me in the face through the entire concert.

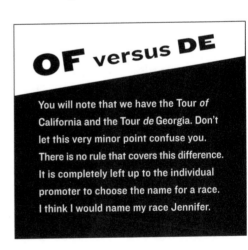

OF versus DE

You will note that we have the Tour *of* California and the Tour *de* Georgia. Don't let this very minor point confuse you. There is no rule that covers this difference. It is completely left up to the individual promoter to choose the name for a race. I think I would name my race Jennifer.

THE LOCAL SCENE

To answer one of the most frequently asked questions, no, I will never ride in the Tour de France. If I had a dollar for every time I was asked that question, I would be able to buy the moon and rename it Jamieville. And George will never ride the Tour either. Only professional riders are allowed in that event. To put it another way, if you're a recreational tennis player, your odds of playing at Wimbledon are pretty slim.

The only way for me to enjoy the pain and suffering of a stage race is at the amateur level. With rare exceptions, local stage races throughout the world are limited to four days and are usually born out of the dreams of a superambitious promoter who wishes to go a step further in providing a place for Roadies to race. They offer Roadies the opportunity to use the different skill set that it takes to successfully tackle a stage race. They may be scored on points instead of time. In this case, they may award points to the top twenty-five places in each stage (25 points for first place, 24 points for second place, 1 point for twenty-fifth place).

Because stage races incorporate the two most-difficult-to-watch race formats— the road race and the time trial—they don't get the same attention that single-day events get.

Recalling the duties of the race promoter described in Chapter 10, you can see that putting together a single-day bike race is an enormous task. Let's multiply that workload three or four times. It is a Herculean effort to put together a local or regional stage race for amateur racers. In addition to the complex logistics, the promoter must provide accurate results for every racer in the field every day. And many of these races provide a race for each category and age group. It's just another reason why there are so few stage races in the United States.

SPECTATORS AND SPECTACLE

Watching a stage race requires that we take everything we know about watching individual races and apply that to a stage race. Then add a hotel room and meals because if we're truly dedicated fans, we will want to stick around for more than one day, and that requires us to travel with the race. We'll also want to get our hands on a decent map and a copy of the GC so that we know who the contenders are. That will help us figure out the team tactics as we see the riders pass by on the roadway. Otherwise, a stage race is not too different from the individual races that it comprises.

An interesting side effect of attending a stage race is the bond you form with other spectators. Compared to a football game, for example, where you sit in the

The NOT-SO-OPEN ROAD

One notable difference to point out in the smaller American stage races is that we are likely to see an occasional criterium or circuit race. This is done to improve the watchability of the event. It's also due in part to the promoter's ability to get permission to use public roads and in part to the popularity of the criterium format in the United States.

same seat for the duration, a stage race requires more effort, which in turn creates an air of cooperation among those following it. Standing along the road for hours at a time gives you time to meet cycling fans from around the world. If it's raining, you're probably sharing an umbrella. If it's cold, you're probably lending the folks from Florida your extra jackets.

As a rider, you have army buddy–type relationships with other riders regardless of what teams you belong to because of what you're going through day after day. Compare this to softball or soccer tournaments in which you may interact with other teams on occasion, but for the most part your team is quite insular. In fact, when you're on the field of play, there are only two teams mixing it up at any one time, and you may never see the same team twice.

A stage race is an extended family on an extended vacation. Those people from Florida you lent the jackets to yesterday will likely be saving you a spot at the finish line of tomorrow's mountain stage. Let's hope they bring some oranges with them!

FINAL LAP

Finally, I need to share this notion: With all the preparation involved—training, nutrition, tactics, recovery, and mechanical considerations, not to mention the mental game—a stage race at any level and of any length is one of the most difficult sporting events to win. Having every element come together to form the perfect storm is a lot to hope for. It makes no difference whether the winner receives worldwide attention and endorsement contracts or, as in the case of most Roadies, a $50 gift certificate to the local steak house; the true champion is easy to find in a stage race. Perhaps that's why it possesses an exalted status among race formats.

The $50 gift certificate will likely be framed and hung above the fireplace.

16. Podium Finish

After a long day at a bike race, Roadies don't just pack up their stuff and head for home after the race. There are a few things they have to do before they hit the road.

Immediately after the race, many riders lapse into what I refer to as the post-race mingle. That's when they all stand around in the street and talk about what just happened. They sip fluids from their water bottles and laugh and joke and rehash the race from every conceivable angle (and again in the car on the way home from the race). This mingling takes on the appearance of a cocktail party. Just so you're prepared, I've seen this party carry on for more than an hour in a steady rain. If you're in a hurry to get home, this portion of the program may frustrate you.

THE AWARDS CEREMONY

Depending on the size and stature of the event, the awards ceremony may be a colorful affair involving a real podium, a bouquet of flowers, an oversized check, and a trophy. On the other hand, it may be nothing more than a handshake and a wave. Either way, a Roadie's role in the awards ceremony is simple: Clean up, show up, and speak up.

Ideally, the top three finishers will be allowed a moment to clean up, drink some water, and put on a clean jersey and a cap. If George makes it to this point, he should patiently await his turn for the announcer to interview him in front of the

adoring fans. He should be prepared with some well-chosen words of congratulation to the other competitors, thanks to the many sponsors (both the race sponsors and his own sponsors), and thanks to the crowd for attending. He will also be asked to describe his winning effort. He should keep it simple for the benefit of those people in the audience who haven't yet read this book.

He should always remember that he is a walking billboard and a live representative for every one of his sponsors. He may never eat at Louie's Restaurant, but if that's the name that's printed on his jersey, then he had better convince people that he eats at Louie's every single night. If not, Louie might decide to pull his money out of the sport of cycling and sponsor a coed softball team instead.

Riders need to realize that the awards ceremony isn't about them as much as it's about the spectators, sponsors, and the sport.

FOR THOSE NOT INVITED TO THE PROM

If George isn't involved with the awards ceremony, then he'll have some extra time on his hands. The first thing he should do after the race is check the results for accuracy. If there's a discrepancy in the finishing order, George will need to file a protest with the officials. If not, he will have some time to "warm down" by riding a few slow miles. (In many parts of the United States, this is referred to as a "cool-down." I have no idea why that is. It just is.) Many riders feel that this step is just as important as the pre-race warm-up. Others skip it. Hey, it's a free country.

WHAT YOU CAN DO

If a Roadie you know wins a trip to the awards ceremony, you can save the day by waiting at the finish line with a towel, cold water, sports drink, clean jersey, cap, and camera. Thrust the towel into his hands. Pour water on his arms, face, hands, and legs. Advise him on how to use the towel. Wash the road grime, drool, and sweat off his face. Pull the cap onto his head. Hold his bike for him and push him in the direction of the announcer. Take a picture of him on the podium holding the flowers and raising his hands in the air. This is what it's all about.

The Roadie's sponsor should receive a copy of this photo. Make sure it's in focus.

The warm-/cool-down ride needn't last more than ten or fifteen minutes. It entails doing nothing more than riding slowly, drinking lots of water, and discussing how someone else messed up your chances of winning the race.

Being mindful of the fifteen-minute protest period, George will want to gravitate toward the results posting area to discuss any protests that might arise. I consider this to be part of the race. In other words, the race ain't over until the money is paid. This process seldom takes more than five minutes. It behooves George to stick around and wait for the results to be finalized.

KEEPING CLEAN

I've heard differing opinions on what a rider should do immediately following the race and subsequent warm-down, but I believe the first order of business should be to change clothes and remove the cycling shorts as soon as possible. Following intense exercise, a humid environment grows in the cycling shorts that can become a breeding ground for fungal problems evolving into sores and boils on the part of the body that usually rests on the saddle. Keeping this area clean and dry is essential to proper hygiene and should be the first thing done after the completion of a race.

MASSAGE BOARD

Ask any Roadie about the importance of massage, and he'll tell you it's key to proper recovery. Somewhere in this post-race melee, then, you should spend time rubbing your legs. Do this at your convenience, but do it before your legs turn to concrete from lactic-acid buildup.

Some riders prefer to whine about how sore their legs are. To heighten this effect and provide more fuel for whining, they will skip the massage.

TO THE BATMOBILE, ROBIN!

One of the next steps should be to pack everything back into the car and make sure everything is accounted for. Earlier I said there's nothing worse than forgetting to bring something to the bike race. I was holding back. In truth, there's nothing worse than losing stuff at a bike race.

This process can be lengthy. Invariably, another rider will roll by and engage in a lengthy conversation much like the previous one that required a complete retelling of the race. Again, this is one of the social aspects of the sport that riders enjoy. This is common in almost every sport and must be accepted as a part of the scene. (I'm generalizing. Obviously, not all Roadies will kill an entire day at a bike race—just 97 percent of them.)

After everything is back where it belongs, it's always a good idea for a Roadie to find the promoter and thank him for making the race possible. Most well-intentioned riders probably think about doing this, but many never actually turn thought into deed. The promoter and volunteers have put their lives on hold in order to put this bike race together. They appreciate hearing positive feedback from the participants, and it helps them decide whether or not to go through the trouble again next summer.

Another important and powerful action is to find and thank the sponsors for footing the bill for the event. If they are not on-site, then each Roadie should write a letter of thanks within the following month. This may seem like common sense, but only a few riders actually take the time to seek out the sponsors and show their appreciation for the contribution made to their favorite sport. This small gesture goes a long, long way in building a good name for the sport of bike racing. There are so many other sports that sponsors can get involved in. We should thank them often for choosing ours.

DAY IS DONE, GONE THE SUN

When the race is over, the gear is packed, and the drive home is under way, the Roadie goes through the debriefing/rehashing phase. This

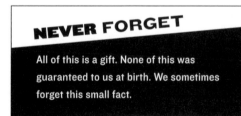

NEVER FORGET

All of this is a gift. None of this was guaranteed to us at birth. We sometimes forget this small fact.

is valuable for the Roadie but can be painful for everyone within earshot. Roadies tend to dissect every race mile by mile, lap by lap, pedal stroke by pedal stroke, until they've said everything three or four times in three or four different ways. They replay what happened at critical points in the race. They retell the story of how they avoided a crash. They describe the sprint in super slo-mo. They have a handful of reasons why they weren't able to place in the prize money. They give a full account of the race through the eyes of each one of their teammates.

SOME DAYS ARE DIAMONDS . . .

If you opted out of the daylong trip to a thirty-minute bike race and missed the big show, then the best question to ask a Roadie when he returns home from a bike race is, Want to grab a bite to eat?

The answer will probably be yes, but if he responds in a positive tone, then it's probably safe to ask about the race. If he responds with a grunt or a snort, then you are not obligated to press him for an answer. Instead, just wait. He'll open up sooner or later.

A Roadie may go through a wide array of moods in the hours following a bike race. I've traveled with a lot of different riders, and I've seen a lot of different behaviors. Generally, Roadies are a fairly self-realized group of athletes who understand that real life greets us as we pull into the driveway. However, some riders take the result of a bike race too seriously. It's nothing a little forgiveness and a gentle nudge back in the direction of reality can't cure. Roadies often push themselves far past the point of collapse and come away with nothing. That can be horribly frustrating.

That, my friends, is bike racing.

HEY! WE'RE ON THE COURSE

Don't be surprised if, many years later while driving with a Roadie through a strange town in an out-of-the-way location, he gets excited for no apparent reason and blurts out, "Hey! We're on the course!"

He means that he once raced his bike on that particular street sometime in his life. It may have been ten years ago, but Roadies remember every turn and every feature of every course they've ever ridden, and they will recognize the course as they drive through town.

To everyone else, it will look like an ordinary town. That is, it has a bank, a post office, a movie theater, and a grocery store. To the Roadie, though, it is and always will be a racecourse and nothing else. Not only that, but he will probably insist on driving a lap of the course while providing a recap of what happened. Let me warn you that, just as he did on the day of the race, he will again provide you with a pedal-stroke-by-pedal-stroke account of what happened during the race. It doesn't matter if the race happened last week or during the Nixon administration. His memory of the event will be astoundingly clear. This is a normal part of the process. It's like having a fantastic meal at a fancy restaurant and taking a doggy bag home with you. You get to heat it up and enjoy it all over again. Roadies reheat the same meal over and over again.

FINAL LAP

Who would have guessed that a Roadie would come with an instruction manual? Certainly, when viewed from curbside, a bike race looks rather simple, so it's natural to assume that a Roadie's life is simple, too. We now know that's not the case. Bike racing is a complex, multilayered sport that, once allowed to dig its hooks into its participants, completely dominates all aspects of a Roadie's life. There is no dabbling in bike racing.

EPILOGUE

If There's a Better Sport, We Haven't Found It

Just as a bike race provides fodder for conversation and contemplation, there is little about the culture of cycling that isn't fascinating, exciting, or worthy of admiration. And spectators fall for the sport as passionately as Roadies do.

Everything I've written about in this book acts as a strong glue that holds Roadies firmly in place. We have each found a magnetic attraction to this sport. As I mentioned in the first chapter, it's far easier to convince even the most indifferent onlooker that there is something likable about bike racing than it is to pry a Roadie away from his sport.

As a spectator, it's easy to find your place in the bike racing scene and support your Roadie friends—and I have some final thoughts on how you can go about it. If you are having visions of shiny road bikes in your future, stay tuned for some final notes for delving into your new life as a Roadie.

FRIENDS, ROMANS, FAMILY MEMBERS

Attend a race. Whatever preconceived notion you have of this bizarre sport can be thrown out the window. There are so many different things going on in any given bike race that you're sure to find something to like about it. If you're alert, you will discover many things I didn't include in this book.

Don't remind a Roadie that he should be looking for a job. A friend of mine graduated from college with a degree in business. While his classmates entered the workforce, he spent the summer racing his bike. His parents constantly pestered him to find a job and begin his career. As summer went by, they put enormous pressure on him to "get back on track." Eventually the season ended, and my friend found a great job. He still races his bike. He still has the job. It all worked out.

Have no fear about the future; bike racers tend to be successful in whatever endeavor they choose because they know what it means to be dedicated. They have a work ethic that has been shaped by participation in a very demanding sport that doesn't favor shortcuts.

Don't label a Roadie as selfish. Bike racing is a demanding pursuit that comes across as egocentric. A Roadie may skip a birthday party or family outing if it falls on the same day as a bike race, but he loves his friends and family nonetheless. He may be unavailable every Tuesday night from March to October. Please look at it another way. He also loves racing bikes and has a finite window of opportunity to compete at his best.

Appreciate the fact that your Roadie has a passion for something and isn't just a potato parked in front of the TV seven nights a week. I encourage you to find a passion that makes such rigorous demands of you physically, creatively, emotionally, or intellectually. This makes your life richer and therefore makes us all more interesting.

Don't make fun of a Roadie because he chose a different sport. Maybe he can't relate to everyone else who is talking about the National League pennant race. So? So he shaves his legs. So? So he dresses up in a suit but wears cycling socks underneath. So? Variety is the spice of life. If you want mainstream, go mainstream. Just know that a lot of people wish they had the temerity to take the road less traveled but are trapped in the everyday.

Ask a Roadie to tell you a story. Of his worst Bonk. Of his best race. Of his favorite training route. Of his worst day in the saddle. Of how he got into the sport. Of his first racing bicycle. You'll learn more about the sport, and you'll be infected by his enthusiasm.

Don't worry about how expensive the sport is. Yes, cycling ranks somewhere near yachting and racehorses, but as long as your Roadie can make his car payment on time, there shouldn't be a problem. Sure, it would be cheaper to be a runner; they only need shoes and shorts. But cheap isn't what this is about.

A Roadie can't be rushed through his race day routine. As I mentioned in Chapter 3, this is a lifestyle, not a dental appointment. It's about the scene and the feeling of belonging to a larger thing. (A thirty-minute criterium burns up an entire day.) It can be annoying when someone pushes you through a routine at a faster pace than you're prepared for. Here's a far-fetched example: Whenever I'm watching Michigan lose the Rose Bowl, I like to immerse myself in the occasion and stay in it until the last seconds have ticked off the clock, especially if the game is exciting. But invariably, during the fourth quarter, the commentators will interrupt the moment by reminding us, "Coming up on CBS, stay tuned for *60 Minutes,* followed by an all-new episode of *Murder, She Wrote.*"

I know that life continues after the game, but I don't want to be reminded of it. It spoils the magic of the moment. Likewise, during a fantastic weekend of bike racing, most Roadies don't want to hear someone say, "Oh, man, I have so much work to do at the office tomorrow." Zip it! Don't ruin the moment by talking about tomorrow. We're at a bike race now.

Make friends with others in the community. Roadies come from all walks of life, and they bring their friends with them. Surely you will find someone you can connect with at a bike race. There's not a bad person among them. Do this, and in no time you will have your own reasons for wanting to spend your weekends watching a bike race.

Learn about the history of the sport. You'll be captivated. It is a sport with a glorious past. The NFL has the frozen tundra days of the Green Bay Packers. Major League Baseball has the Yankees and Red Sox. The NHL has the Original Six. Soccer has the World Cup. Tennis has Bjorn, John, Jimmy, Arthur, Chrissie, and Martina.

Cycling has all that and more. There are plenty of books to read and videotapes to watch that tell the story of this very cool sport.

When you go to a bike race, always take a batch of chocolate-chip cookies for the announcer.

FOR PARTICIPANTS NEW AND OLD

Anytime you are on your bike, remember that you are an ambassador for our beloved sport of cycling. Worldwide acceptance was not granted to us at the dawn of time. Many riders who have gone before you have worked hard to win the hearts of Americans. Don't blow it for us.

Never complain. The world hates a whiner. We all know that bike racing is not a perfect sport, but action, not words, is what it takes to improve it. There will be times when you find yourself in a negative situation. Always handle these situations with grace and aplomb. That way, if the outcome is not to your liking, at least you won't make a fool of yourself.

Develop an interest in something other than cycling. You'll be less dull in social situations because you won't be talking about cycling 24/7.

Take the time to thank the people around you who make it possible for you to ride and race your bike. Team sponsors, race promoters, event volunteers, family members, and anyone else you can think of. Thank them, and mean it when you say it.

Support your friends in their endeavors as they support you in yours. Fake it if you have to. Chances are, they're faking it when they come to a bike race.

Share the sport with a youngster. Start planting seeds for the future.

Volunteer to help at a bike race. Spend some time working on the other side of the hay bales to learn what makes an event tick. It will give you a better appreciation for those who make your race happen, as well as a broader perspective on race day.

Travel to the Tour de France. Sleep on a picnic table. Paint your favorite rider's name on the road. Eat baguettes. Drink warm Coke. Scream like an idiot when the peloton flies by. Life's short. Live it up!

If you are an aspiring Roadie, get ready to defend your choice of sports to all of your friends, relatives, and coworkers. They'll have questions.

I'll say it again: chocolate-chip cookies for the announcer. Let's not make it more complicated than it needs to be.

SEE YOU AT THE RACES

One of my favorite aspects of the sport is the people who make up this close-knit community. I think most Roadies would echo my sentiments. We point to a lot of reasons that explain our involvement in the sport: speed, tactics, equipment, travel, and so on. But what truly reels us in are the friends and acquaintances we spend time with every weekend during the summer. No matter where we go, we see the same supportive group of people who share our interest, enthusiasm, and dedication. How awesome is that?

This is what John Howard means by "seasonal unions" and "lasting friendships." Though we compete against each other on the bikes, we are one big family off the bike. This is the real hook that keeps us coming back again and again; without it, we're just a bunch of cyclists riding around in circles.

ABOUT THE AUTHOR

Jamie Smith has been avoided at family reunions and company picnics since 1984, shortly after he became a bike racer. Since then, he has lived on both ends of cycling's spectrum. He has been a bike racer since 1983, working his way up through the ranks of amateur cycling, and a bike race announcer since 1985, traveling with some of the world's greatest cyclists.

Ever a zealot, Smith has gotten fired for calling in sick to attend a bike race, and he has slept in his car for four days to be able to volunteer at the Tour de Michigan.

Putting all his experiences together, he has written a book to help his family and his coworkers understand why he has become so entrenched in a strange, expensive, complicated, quirky, demanding, and misunderstood sport. Smith originally embarked upon *Roadie* as a means of dumping cycling out of his brain forever to make room for new activities such as golf, tennis, and a social life. But the more he wrote, the more he realized that cycling inspires a stubborn kind of love.

A graduate of Central Michigan University's Broadcast and Cinematic Arts program, Smith has become adept at describing cycling's most complex intricacies to normal people. Today he is still avoided at company picnics, but he has made considerable progress with his family.

ABOUT THE ILLUSTRATOR

Jef Mallett grew up in a family of musicians and teachers, and right from the start, he spent a lot of time around creative chaos and a thirst for learning. When he was fifteen years old, he started drawing a daily comic strip for the Big Rapids Pioneer, and he continued it until he graduated in 1980.

Frazz, Mallett's comic strip, has been in newspapers nationwide for seven years. That's a while for a guy with Mallett's attention span but about right when you consider that his first daily comic strip was published thirty-two years ago, when he was in high school. Cementing its status in modern culture, *Frazz* has been mentioned in *Newsweek* and in a cover story in *USA Triathlon Life*, quoted in Ann Landers's advice column, and—yes—been an answer on *Jeopardy! Frazz* won the Religion Communicators Council's Wilbur award for excellence in portraying ethics, values, and religion in the secular media in 2003 and 2005. It was a finalist for the National Cartoonists Society's 2005 Reuben award for best comic strip.

In addition to his comic strip, Mallett is the author of a children's book, a contributing editor to *Inside Triathlon* magazine, and a contributing artist to *VeloNews* magazine.

Mallett raced in his first triathlon in 1981 but only rarely has to worry about looking nice for the awards ceremony. After a miserable swim and remarkable bike split in his first race, he got the hint and took up bicycle racing. Since then, Mallett has bounced back and forth between sports, regularly logging long, hard days on two wheels.

Mallett lives in Lansing, Michigan, with his wife, Patty.